MAXIMIZE YOUR PODCAST FOR LOW COST

Maximize Your Podcast for Low Cost

DAKOTA FRANDSEN

Bald and Bonkers Network LLC

First Printing, 2023

ISBN: 978-1-0881-5389-5 (paperback)
978-1-0881-5396-3 (ebook)

Contents

Dedicated to the Bald and Bonkers Network Academy Students

This book was made to go with an online course of the same name offered by Bald and Bonkers Network LLC

To visit the course, go to:
https://bald-and-bonkers-network-academy.teachable.com/p/
maximize-your-podcast-for-low-cost

Chapter 1

Introduction

Picture this: You're sitting in a dimly lit room, head-phones on, staring at your computer screen with anticipation. The countdown begins, and suddenly, you hear it. The smooth, melodic voice of your favorite podcaster fills your ears, transporting you to another world. You're hooked, and you want to be a part of this magical world of podcasting.

But there's one problem. You're on a tight budget. You don't have the funds to invest in expensive equipment or hire a team of professionals to help you. You're just a regular person with a passion for sharing your thoughts and ideas with the world.

Well, my friend, I have some great news for you. In this book, "Maximize Your Podcast for Low Cost," I will show you how to start and run a podcast/

webshow without breaking the bank. That's right – you can join the ranks of successful podcasters and webshow hosts without emptying your wallet.

Now, you might be thinking, "How is that even possible?" Well, let me tell you. I've spent years in the world of podcasting and webshow hosting, and I've learned a thing or two about maximizing resources and minimizing costs. In this book, I will share with you my tried-and-true strategies for starting a podcast, hosting a podcast, starting a webshow, and so much more – all on a shoestring budget.

Whether you're a seasoned podcaster looking to cut down on expenses or a complete newbie wondering where to start, this book is for you. I will guide you through every step of the process, from choosing the right equipment to landing high-profile guests and engaging your audience. You'll learn how to design a captivating logo and intro that will leave a lasting impression on your listeners. And, of course, we'll dive into the world of monetization, because let's face it – we all want to make a little extra cash from our passion projects.

But this book is not just about saving money – it's about maximizing your potential. I firmly believe that with the right mindset and a solid plan, anyone can create a successful podcast or webshow. And that's exactly what I want to help you achieve. I want to empower you to share your unique voice with the world, to captivate an audience and make a difference.

In the pages ahead, I will guide you through every step of the process, from conceptualizing your podcast or webshow idea to launching it with a bang. But before we dive into the practical aspects, let's take a moment to explore the power of sharing your unique voice and the impact it can have on the world.

We live in a time where technology has opened up incredible opportunities for anyone with a passion and a voice. The digital age has shattered the barriers that once stood between creators and their audiences, allowing for unprecedented levels of connection and influence. No longer do you need to rely on traditional media outlets to amplify your message or seek validation from gatekeepers who may not understand or appreciate your distinct perspective.

In this age of endless possibilities, your voice matters more than ever. Each person has a unique set of experiences, skills, and insights that can resonate with others in profound ways. By sharing your voice through a podcast or webshow, you have the ability to touch lives, challenge assumptions, and inspire change on a global scale.

But let's not forget that making a difference begins with captivating an audience. In the noisy landscape of the digital world, it can be daunting to stand out from the crowd. That's why I have dedicated an entire section of this book to helping you craft compelling content that speaks directly to your target audience. From choosing the right format to mastering story-telling techniques, I will equip you with the tools you need to captivate, engage, and retain your listeners or viewers.

However, creating a successful podcast or web-show is not just about attracting an audience; it's also about making a lasting impact. We will explore how to establish your brand, build a community around your content, and leverage your platform to drive positive change. Whether you aspire to bring aware-ness to social issues, share your expertise, or enter-tain and uplift others, this book will help you create a blueprint for maximizing your potential and achieving your goals.

In the following chapters, we will deep dive into the technical aspects of podcasting and webshow production. From setting up the necessary equipment to navigating hosting platforms and promoting your content effectively, you will gain a comprehensive understanding of the tools and strategies required to launch and sustain your endeavor.

Remember, this book is not just a step-by-step manual; it is a source of inspiration and motivation.

Alongside practical advice, I will share stories of individuals who have transformed their passions into thriving podcast and webshow projects. Their journeys will serve as a reminder that you, too, have the ability to make a difference by sharing your unique voice with the world.

So, are you ready to embark on this transformative journey? Let's uncover your potential and unleash your voice, one episode at a time. Together, we can create a society where diverse voices are celebrated, ideas are exchanged freely, and positive change becomes the norm. With determination, dedication, and the knowledge contained within these pages, there is no limit to what you can achieve. It's time to make your mark and let your voice be heard.

So, if you're ready to take your podcast or webshow to the next level without breaking the bank, then buckle up, my friend. We're about to embark on an exciting journey together. Get ready to maximize your podcast for low cost and unleash your full potential. Let's dive in!

Chapter 2

Introduction to Podcasting and Webshows

1.1: Understanding Podcasting

This subchapter is all about diving into the world of podcasting and unraveling its fascinating history, as well as understanding the reasons why it has become such a popular medium of communication and entertainment. So, grab your headphones and let's embark on this audio adventure!

Imagine a world where you can listen to your favorite shows and stories whenever and wherever you want. A world where you can immerse yourself in captivating conversations, learn new things, and be entertained on your own terms. Welcome to the wonderful world of podcasting!

But what exactly is podcasting? Well, think of it as the lovechild of radio and the internet. Podcasting is the art of creating audio content that is made available for download or streaming online. It's like having your very own radio station that caters to your specific interests and preferences. Whether you're into true crime, comedy, self-help, or anything in between, there's a podcast out there just waiting for you.

Now, let's rewind a bit and explore the history of podcasting. Believe it or not, podcasting has been around for longer than you might think. It all began back in the early 2000s when a group of tech-savvy individuals started experimenting with ways to distribute audio files online. They wanted to create a platform that would allow anyone to share their thoughts and ideas with the world, without the limitations of traditional radio broadcasting.

One of the pioneers of podcasting was Adam Curry, a former MTV VJ, who co-created the first-ever podcasting software called iPodder. This groundbreaking invention allowed users to automatically download and sync audio files to their iPods (hence the name "podcasting"). Soon after, the term "podcast" was coined, and a revolution was born.

So, why has podcasting become such a sensation? Well, there are a few key reasons. First and foremost, podcasts offer a level of freedom and flexibility that traditional media simply can't match. You can listen to a podcast while commuting, doing household chores, or even during your workouts. It's like having a personal DJ in your pocket, ready to entertain you at any given moment.

Additionally, podcasts have become a haven for niche interests and diverse voices. Unlike mainstream media, which often caters to the masses, podcasts allow for a more intimate and personalized listening experience. You can find shows on virtually any topic imaginable, from knitting to astrophysics to conspiracy theories about time-traveling cats. The possibilities are endless!

Furthermore, the rise of podcasting has been fueled by the democratization of technology. Gone are the days when you needed expensive broadcasting equipment or a record deal to create your own show. With just a decent microphone and a laptop, anyone can become a podcaster and share their unique perspective with the world. This accessibility has opened doors for underrepresented voices and untold stories to be heard.

Now, let's address the elephant in the room - why are podcasts so addictive? Well, it's partly due to the intimate nature of the medium. When you listen to a podcast, it feels like you're having a conversation with the hosts or guests. You become a part of their world, as they share their thoughts, experiences, and even their quirks. It's like eavesdropping on a captivating discussion between friends, but without the guilt.

But wait, there's more! Podcasts also provide a

sense of community and connection. Through social media and online forums, listeners can engage with their favorite hosts and fellow fans. It's like joining a secret club where you can geek out over your shared interests and exchange recommendations for new shows to binge-listen.

So, there you have it - a crash course in understanding podcasting. We've explored its history, delved into the reasons behind its popularity, and uncovered the secrets of its addictive allure. Now that you have a solid grasp of the podcasting landscape, it's time to take the plunge and start exploring the vast ocean of audio content. Just remember, the only side effect of podcast addiction is an insatiable thirst for knowledge and a never-ending playlist.

As you embark on this exhilarating journey of podcast exploration, prepare to be captivated by a kaleidoscope of voices and stories that will transport you to realms both real and imagined. Whether you find solace in true crime mysteries that send shivers down your spine, or prefer the soothing serenade of a meditation podcast guiding you to inner peace, the world of podcasting holds a treasure trove of captivating tales waiting to be discovered.

With each new episode, you will become immersed in the intimate conversations of hosts who share their wisdom, laughter, and vulnerabilities as if you were sitting right beside them. You will become part of a global community, connected by a shared passion for knowledge and an insatiable curiosity.

As you dive deeper into the vast ocean of audio content, you will encounter shows that enlighten and challenge your beliefs, leaving you pondering the complexities of the human condition. You may stumble upon hidden gems that transport you to far-off lands, revealing cultures and perspectives different from your own, fostering empathy and understanding.

But the power of podcasting extends beyond mere entertainment. It equips you with the tools to expand your horizons, enrich your mind, and nourish your soul. You'll uncover interviews with trailblazers who have conquered adversity, inspiring you to embrace your own potential and chase your dreams unabashedly.

In this realm, time is no longer a constraint. A single swipe can transport you from a bustling metropolis to the heart of nature's wilderness. You can explore the realms of science, history, literature, and politics —all with the freedom to pause, rewind, and savor the moments that resonate most deeply.

And as you lose yourself in the captivating narratives woven by skilled storytellers, let the world fade away, allowing yourself to be fully present in the moment. Savor the laughter, the tears, and the profound wisdom that only a truly exceptional podcast can elicit. For here, in this digital sanctuary of sound, you will find enlightenment and inspiration.

So, my intrepid listener, let the passion for knowledge guide your choices, for the world of podcasting beckons you with open arms. Embrace the endless possibilities that await in the realm of audio story-telling. May your playlist be rich, diverse, and ever-expanding, and may your journey through the sea of podcasts be nothing short of extraordinary. Happy listening!

1.2: Exploring Webshows

In this exciting subchapter, we dive headfirst into the world of webshows and unravel their unique features that set them apart from traditional podcasts. So grab your popcorn and get ready for a thrilling ride!

Imagine a podcast, but with visuals that make you feel like you're right there in the room with the hosts. That's the magic of webshows! These digital marvels take the traditional podcasting experience and sprinkle it with a pinch of video magic, creating a dynamic and engaging form of content.

Webshows have exploded in popularity, and for good reason. They offer a whole new level of entertainment by combining the power of audio with the captivating visuals of video. It's like having the best of both worlds, and who doesn't love that?

One of the biggest advantages of webshows is their ability to reach a wider audience. While podcasts rely solely on audio, webshows have the potential to capture the attention of visual learners and those who crave a more immersive experience. So if you're looking to expand your podcast's reach and captivate a larger audience, webshows are the way to go.

But what exactly makes webshows different from traditional podcasts? Well, for starters, it's all about the visual aspect. Webshows allow hosts to showcase their vibrant personalities and engage with their audience through expressive facial expressions and gestures. It adds a whole new layer of depth to the content and creates a stronger connection with viewers.

Another key feature of webshows is the incorporation of visuals, such as graphics, images, and even live demonstrations. This visual feast not only enhances the overall viewing experience but also aids in conveying complex concepts or demonstrating how-to processes. So whether you're explaining the intricacies of astrophysics or showcasing a mouthwatering recipe, webshows provide the perfect platform to bring your ideas to life.

Now, you might be wondering how webshows differ from other video content, like YouTube videos or TV shows. Well, webshows have a unique charm that sets them apart. Unlike TV shows, webshows have a more casual and conversational tone, allowing hosts to connect with their audience on a personal level. And unlike YouTube videos, webshows are typically longer and dive deeper into specific topics, providing a more comprehensive and in-depth experience.

Webshows also offer the incredible opportunity to create a loyal and engaged community. With the power of social media and live chats, hosts can interact with their audience in real-time, answering questions, addressing comments, and fostering a sense of belonging. It's like having your very own virtual hangout where you can connect with like-minded individuals who share your passion.

Now that you understand the unique features of webshows, let's talk about their potential. Webshows have the power to take your podcast to new heights by reaching a wider audience and captivating viewers with their immersive experience. So if you're ready to level up your content creation game, it's time to explore the world of webshows and unleash your creative genius!

Remember, the possibilities are endless with webshows. You can showcase your expertise, entertain and educate, or simply have a blast with your cohosts. So grab your camera, put on your director's hat, and get ready to create a webshow that will leave your audience craving for more!With a passionate sparkle in her eyes, Emily took a deep breath and stepped onto the brightly lit set. The whirring of the cameras and the gentle hush from the crew filled the air, heightening her excitement and igniting her creativity.

This was the moment she had been waiting for - the moment to bring her webshow dream to life.

As the music swelled and the set came alive with vibrant colors, Emily felt the adrenaline rush through her veins. She was determined to make her webshow a captivating experience, one that would leave her viewers enchanted and coming back for more. She knew deep down that this was her opportunity to change the world, one episode at a time.

Her webshow, aptly named "Unleash Your Inner Wonder," was not just about entertainment but also about inspiring others to embrace their passions and discover their hidden talents. Emily knew that within each person's soul lay a world of untapped potential, waiting to be unleashed. And through her webshow, she aimed to ignite that fire within her audience, empowering them to chase their dreams fearlessly.

With her trusted co-hosts by her side, Emily began brainstorming ideas. They decided to blend education with entertainment, creating a perfect balance that would captivate a wide range of viewers. From showcasing DIY projects to exploring the wonders of nature, each episode would be a magical journey of discovery and personal growth.

Emily's love for storytelling took center stage as she meticulously crafted each script, leaving no detail overlooked. Intriguing plot twists, heartwarming anecdotes, and relatable characters filled the storyline with depth and substance. The interplay between her co-hosts was natural and infectious, making every episode a delightful dance of camaraderie and wit.

But Emily's vision extended beyond the screen. She wanted her webshow to become a community - a platform where viewers could share their own stories, seek advice, and ignite conversations. Through social media platforms and regular live streams, Emily fostered an inclusive environment, embracing diversity and applauding individuality. She encouraged her viewers to participate, knowing that their unique voices could amplify the reach and impact of their collective message.

Week after week, "Unleash Your Inner Wonder" grew in popularity, capturing the hearts and minds of viewers from every corner of the globe. Inspired by the webshow's magic, many took bold steps towards their dreams, creating their own webshows, writing novels, or starting a business.

As Emily reflected on the overwhelming success of her webshow, she realized that the possibilities truly were endless. Beyond the fame and recognition, it was the positive impact she had made that filled her heart with joy. She had created a community of dreamchasers, a tribe united in their pursuit of a life filled with purpose and limitless possibilities.

With tears of gratitude streaming down her face, Emily whispered, "Thank you, world, for believing in the power of webshows. Thank you for joining me on this incredible journey. And remember, the choice to embrace your inner wonder is always within your grasp. So, go ahead, create, inspire, and let the world witness your magic!"

And now, for a little joke to lighten the mood. Why did the podcaster start a webshow? Because they wanted to "cast" a wider net and reel in more viewers! So get ready to cast your webshow into the vast ocean of content creation and watch as your audience grows like a school of excited fish!

In the next subchapter, we'll explore the exciting world of low-cost maintenance and promotion for your webshow, so stay tuned for more insightful tips and tricks. Happy webshow creating!

1.3: Identifying Target Audience

In this subchapter, we dive deep into the crucial task of identifying your target audience. You may be wondering, "Why is it so important to know my audience?" Well, dear reader, the answer is simple – knowing your audience is the key to creating engaging content that resonates with them.

Think about it this way: if you were a chef creating a

delicious dish, wouldn't you want to know who you're cooking for? You wouldn't serve a juicy steak to a group of vegetarians, would you? The same principle applies to content creation. By understanding your audience's interests, niche, and content preferences, you can serve up the perfect dish of engaging content that leaves them hungry for more.

So, let's get started on the journey of identifying your target audience. First and foremost, you need to ask yourself who would be interested in your podcast or webshow. Is it tech-savvy individuals who love exploring the latest gadgets and gizmos? Is it science fiction enthusiasts who crave mind-bending stories set in futuristic worlds? Or perhaps it's students who are eager to learn and stay updated with the latest technological advancements.

Once you have a general idea of who your audience might be, it's time to dig deeper and get to know them on a more personal level. Consider their age, gender, occupation, and hobbies. Are they tech-savvy millennials who spend their days immersed in the world of social media, or are they seasoned professionals looking to expand their knowledge in the tech and science fiction realms? Understanding these demographic details will help you tailor your content to their specific needs and interests.

But wait, there's more! In the age of the internet, it's essential to consider your audience's online behavior. Are they active on social media platforms like Instagram, Twitter, or Reddit? Do they prefer listening to podcasts during their daily commute or watching webshows during their lunch breaks? Understanding how your audience consumes content will allow you to reach them where they're most likely to engage with your work.

Now, here's a pro tip for you: don't be afraid to get personal with your audience. Engaging content is all about building a connection and fostering a sense of community. Ask your audience questions, encourage them to share their thoughts and opinions, and create spaces where they can interact with you and each other. This not only helps you understand your audience better but also creates a loyal and dedicated following.

Finally, let's talk about the importance of constant feedback and adaptation. Your audience is not a static entity – they are ever-evolving and so should your content. Keep a keen eye on analytics, track engagement, and listen to your audience's feedback. This will allow you to identify what works and what doesn't, giving you the power to adapt and grow.

Remember, dear reader, identifying your target audience is like putting on a pair of glasses – it brings everything into focus. By understanding who you're creating content for, you can ensure that your podcast or webshow becomes a must-listen or must-watch for your audience. So, go forth and conquer the realm of content creation with this newfound knowledge!

And now, for a little joke to lighten the mood: Why did the webshow host go to the eye doctor? Because they needed help identifying their target audience – their vision was a little blurry!

In this subchapter, we dive deep into the crucial task of identifying your target audience. You may be wondering, "Why is it so important to know my audience?" Well, dear reader, the answer is simple – knowing your audience is the key to creating engaging content that resonates with them.

Think about it this way: if you were a chef creating a delicious dish, wouldn't you want to know who you're cooking for? You wouldn't serve a juicy steak to a group of vegetarians, would you? The same principle applies to content creation. By understanding your audience's interests, niche, and content preferences, you can serve up the perfect dish of engaging content that leaves them hungry for more.

So, let's get started on the journey of identifying your target audience. First and foremost, you need to ask yourself who would be interested in your podcast or webshow. Is it tech-savvy individuals who love exploring the latest gadgets and gizmos? Is it science fiction enthusiasts who crave mind-bending stories set in futuristic worlds? Or perhaps it's students who are eager to learn and stay updated with the latest technological advancements.

Once you have a general idea of who your audience might be, it's time to dig deeper and get to know them on a more personal level. Consider their age, gender, occupation, and hobbies. Are they tech-savvy millennials who spend their days immersed in the world of social media, or are they seasoned professionals looking to expand their knowledge in the tech and science fiction realms? Understanding these demographic details will help you tailor your content to their specific needs and interests.

But wait, there's more! In the age of the internet, it's essential to consider your audience's online behavior. Are they active on social media platforms like Instagram, Twitter, or Reddit? Do they prefer listening to podcasts during their daily commute or watching webshows during their lunch breaks? Understanding how your audience consumes content will allow you to reach them where they're most likely to engage with your work.

Now, here's a pro tip for you: don't be afraid to get personal with your audience. Engaging content is all about building a connection and fostering a sense of community. Ask your audience questions, encourage them to share their thoughts and opinions, and create spaces where they can interact with you and each other. This not only helps you understand your audience better but also creates a loyal and dedicated following.

Finally, let's talk about the importance of constant feedback and adaptation. Your audience is not a static entity – they are ever-evolving and so should your content. Keep a keen eye on analytics, track engagement, and listen to your audience's feedback. This will allow you to identify what works and what doesn't, giving you the power to adapt and grow.

Remember, dear reader, identifying your target audience is like putting on a pair of glasses – it brings everything into focus. By understanding who you're creating content for, you can ensure that your podcast or webshow becomes a must-listen or must-watch for your audience. So, go forth and conquer the realm of content creation with this newfound knowledge!

And now, for a little joke to lighten the mood: Why did the webshow host go to the eye doctor? Because they needed help identifying their target audience – their vision was a little blurry!

But fear not, as they walked out of the eye doctor's office with a prescription for clarity, their content creation journey took an extraordinary turn. Armed with their newfound knowledge, they began honing in on their target audience like a skilled archer aiming for the bullseye.

They started by conducting surveys and polls, reaching out to their existing audience, and asking them what they loved most about the show. They also ventured into the vast realms of social media, creating engaging posts and content that resonated with their target audience. And boy, did it pay off!

Their online community began to flourish, with followers eagerly sharing their episodes, leaving comments, and engaging in lively discussions. The webshow host realized that by truly understanding their audience, they could bring them even closer together, fostering a loyal and dedicated following.

But it didn't stop there. The webshow host

recognized the importance of staying ahead of the curve in the ever-evolving world of content creation. They monitored trends, researched emerging topics, and sought out experts to interview on their show. By continuously adapting their content to meet the changing needs and interests of their audience, they became the go-to authority in their niche.

And as their audience grew, so did their impact. They received messages of gratitude from listeners who shared how their show had inspired them to pursue their passions, think critically, and embrace the wonders of technology and science fiction. The webshow host realized the power they held in shaping minds and sparking curiosity within their audience.

With each episode, they aimed to stimulate the imagination, provoke thought, and foster a sense of wonder. Whether it was discussing the ethical implications of artificial intelligence, exploring the possibilities of interplanetary travel, or dissecting the latest technological breakthroughs, their content ignited a fire within their audience, driving them to learn, explore, and dream.

And so, as the webshow host continued on their content creation journey, they remained dedicated to discovering new ways to connect with their audience. They treasured the relationships they built, always seeking feedback, and making adjustments along the way. Through it all, they recognized that identifying their target audience was not just a one-time task but an ongoing commitment to understanding and serving the needs of those who mattered most – their beloved audience.

And in the end, they realized that their success as a content creator was not simply measured by numbers or accolades but by the impact they had on the lives of their audience. For in their hands, they held the power to educate, inspire, and entertain - a responsibility they embraced with passion and unwavering dedication.

So, dear reader, as you embark on your own journey of content creation, remember the importance of knowing your audience. Identify them, understand them, and connect with them in ways that resonate deeply. And may your content become a masterpiece that leaves a lasting impression on the hearts and minds of those who discover it.

1.4: Benefits of Podcasting and Webshows

In this subchapter, we delve into the exciting world of podcasting and webshows and explore the multitude of benefits they bring. From building a personal brand to networking opportunities and establishing authority in a specific field, starting a podcast or web-show opens up a world of possibilities.

One of the primary benefits of podcasting and web-shows is the opportunity to build a personal brand. With the rise of digital media, having a strong personal brand has become crucial. By hosting a podcast or webshow, you can showcase your expertise, personality, and unique perspective to a wide audience. It's like having your own digital soapbox, where you can share your thoughts, ideas, and experiences with the world.

In addition to building a personal brand, podcasting and webshows offer fantastic networking opportunities. When you host a podcast or webshow, you have the chance to connect with industry experts, influencers, and like-minded individuals. Through interviews, collaborations, and guest appearances, you can expand your professional network and open doors to exciting new opportunities. Who knows? Your next guest could be a game-changer in your field or a future collaborator on a groundbreaking project.

Furthermore, podcasting and webshows allow you to establish authority in a specific field. As you consistently produce valuable and insightful content, your audience will come to see you as a trusted source of information and expertise. This credibility can open doors to speaking engagements, consulting opportunities, and even book deals. It's like becoming the go-to person in your niche, the one people turn to for advice, guidance, and inspiration.

But wait, there's more! Podcasting and webshows also offer the chance to engage with your audience in a meaningful way. Through comments, messages, and social media interactions, you can build a community of loyal listeners and viewers who eagerly await your next episode. This sense of connection and engagement is incredibly rewarding, as you witness firsthand the impact your content has on others. Plus, it's a great way to get feedback, suggestions, and ideas for future episodes.

Now, let's address the elephant in the room - monetization. Yes, podcasting and webshows can also be a lucrative endeavor. With the right strategies and a growing audience, you can explore various monetization opportunities such as sponsorships, merchandise sales, paid subscriptions, and even crowdfunding campaigns. While it may take time and effort to reach this stage, the potential for financial success is undoubtedly there.

And here's a bonus benefit - podcasting and webshows provide a creative outlet like no other. Whether you're a natural-born storyteller, a witty conversationalist, or a passionate advocate for a cause, hosting a podcast or webshow allows you to express yourself in a unique and engaging way. It's like having your own platform to share your creativity with the world, all while having a blast doing it.

So, there you have it - the numerous benefits of

starting a podcast or webshow. From building a personal brand to networking opportunities and establishing authority in your field, the opportunities are endless. And who knows, maybe one day, you'll find yourself at the forefront of the podcasting revolution, inspiring and entertaining listeners from all corners of the globe. As they say, the only way to find out is to hit that record button and start sharing your voice with the world. Happy podcasting!As the world's best writer, I want to add a final touch of inspiration to this text:

So, my dear reader, what are you waiting for? Take the leap into the exciting world of podcasting and webshows. Embrace the limitless possibilities that await you. Let your voice be heard, your story be shared, and your expertise be recognized. It doesn't matter if you're a beginner or an experienced professional – there's room for everyone in this ever-evolving space.

Remember, the journey may not always be easy. It will require dedication, consistency, and a willingness to adapt. But with passion and perseverance, you will overcome any obstacles that come your way.

And who knows, your podcast or webshow may become a catalyst for change, inspiring others, and making a positive impact on the world. Your words have the power to reach hearts and minds, to touch lives, and to foster connections across borders and cultures.

So, go forth, dear reader, and let your podcast or webshow be a beacon of hope and inspiration.

Your unique perspective deserves to be shared, your experiences deserve to be heard, and your message deserves to be amplified.

In the realm of podcasting and webshows, the possibilities are endless. Seize this opportunity, and let your voice resonate with the world. The stage is set, the audience awaits, and greatness is within your reach.

Now, go out there and create something extraordinary. The world is waiting for your story.

1.5: Key Concepts Covered in the Book

Welcome to 1.5: Key Concepts Covered in the Book! In this subchapter, we'll give you a sneak peek of the exciting concepts we'll be diving into in the following chapters. Think of it as a tantalizing appetizer before the feast of knowledge that awaits you.

First on the menu is the art of starting a podcast. We'll guide you through the entire process, from choosing the perfect topic to creating engaging content that will hook your listeners from the very first episode. Trust me, after reading this chapter, you'll be itching to grab that microphone and hit record!

Next up, we'll explore the world of hosting. No, not the kind that involves dinner parties and polite small talk, but rather the technical side of podcasting. We'll demystify the different hosting platforms, help you choose the right one for your needs, and ensure your podcast reaches the ears of eager listeners around the globe.

Now, let's talk about something everyone loves: low-cost maintenance. We understand that not everyone has a bottomless budget, so we'll show you how to keep your podcast running smoothly without breaking the bank. From affordable equipment options to clever editing hacks, we've got you covered.

But what good is a podcast if no one knows about it? That's where low-cost promotion comes in. We'll spill the beans on effective marketing strategies that won't drain your wallet. Get ready to harness the power of social media, collaborate with other podcasters, and attract new listeners like a pro.

Engaging an audience is not just about talking into a microphone. It's about building a community, connecting with your listeners, and creating a memorable experience. We'll share tips and tricks to captivate your audience, encourage interaction, and turn them into loyal fans who eagerly anticipate each new episode.

Now, let's get down to the nitty-gritty of monetization. We'll show you how to turn your passion project into a profitable venture. From sponsorship opportunities to merchandise sales, we'll help you navigate the sometimes murky waters of making money from your podcast, all while keeping it authentic and true to your vision.

But wait, there's more! We'll also delve into the world of starting a webshow, maintaining a strong social media presence, landing impressive guests, designing eye-catching logos and intros, and exploring the fascinating intersection of technology and science fiction.

Phew! That's quite a spread of concepts we'll be covering, don't you think? But fear not, we'll guide you through each one with our signature mix of humor, insight, and detailed explanations. So get ready to embark on this podcasting and webshow adventure, armed with the knowledge and confidence to make your mark in the digital world. It's going to be a wild ride, my friend, and we're thrilled to have you along for it!

Remember, starting a podcast or webshow doesn't have to be intimidating or expensive. With the right guidance and a sprinkle of creativity, you can create content that resonates with your audience and leaves them eagerly hitting that play button. So let's dive in and discover the exciting world of podcasting and webshowing together!

But before we begin, let me leave you with a little joke to lighten the mood. Why did the podcaster always carry a microphone? Because they couldn't resist dropping the mic! Stay tuned for more laughs and valuable insights as we embark on this podcasting and webshowing journey together.

Now that we've set the stage for the exciting concepts we'll be exploring in the following chapters, it's time to dig even deeper into the world of podcasting and webshowing. Are you ready to take the leap and become a master of your craft? Buckle up, because we're about to embark on an exhilarating journey of creativity, knowledge, and personal growth.

In the chapter on starting a podcast, we'll not only guide you through the technical aspects but also delve into the art of storytelling. We'll explore different narrative structures, interview techniques, and the power of sound design to truly captivate your audience. No stone will be left unturned as we help you unlock your storytelling potential and bring your podcasting dreams to life.

Now, let's turn our attention to the world of webshows. We'll uncover the secrets of creating visually stunning content that grabs attention and keeps viewers coming back for more. From camera techniques to lighting and editing, you'll become a master of the visual medium. We'll also discuss effective ways to engage with your audience in real-time through live streaming and interactive features, transforming your webshow into an interactive experience.

But of course, no successful podcast or webshow is complete without a strong social media presence. In the age of digital connectivity, we'll show you how to leverage social media platforms to promote your content, engage with your audience, and build a loyal community around your brand. We'll explore strategies that go beyond mere self-promotion and teach you how to genuinely connect with your followers while increasing your reach and impact.

Additionally, we'll delve into the realm of impressive guests. Whether you're fascinated by experts in your field, beloved celebrities, or influential personalities, we'll provide you with valuable insights on how to approach and attract high-profile guests to elevate your podcast or webshow to new heights. We'll teach you how to pitch your ideas, network effectively, and create an environment that entices guests to join you on your digital stage.

And let's not forget about the importance of visually appealing logos and intros. We'll guide you through the process of designing a captivating logo that represents your brand identity and leaves a lasting impression. We'll also explore the world of intros, discussing how to craft an attention-grabbing opening that sets the tone for your podcast or webshow and entices viewers or listeners to stay tuned for more.

As we navigate the technology and science fiction intersection, we'll explore innovative tools, gadgets, and emerging trends in these fields. From virtual reality to artificial intelligence, we'll open your mind to the endless possibilities for creating unique and immersive content that keeps your audience on the edge of their seats.

Throughout this journey, we'll infuse our guidance with a sprinkle of creativity, a dash of inspiration, and a whole lot of practical advice. We believe that everyone has a story to tell, and with the right tools and mindset, you can create content that not only entertains but also enriches the lives of your audience.

So, my friend, grab your microphone, set up your cameras, and get ready to embark on this thrilling adventure. Together, we'll navigate the sometimes challenging waters of podcasting and webshowing, transforming your passion into a powerful force that resonates with people around the world.

Remember, at the heart of it all is your genuine passion and unique perspective. Embrace your creativity, be bold, and let your authenticity shine through. With our guidance and the magic of your imagination, there are no limits to what you can achieve in the captivating world of podcasting and webshowing.

So let's continue this journey together, armed with humor, insight, and a shared vision for a future filled with content that inspires, connects, and captivates. Get ready, my friend. The spotlight awaits you!

Chapter 3

Starting Your Podcast

2.1: Planning Your Podcast

This subchapter is all about getting your creative juices flowing and laying the groundwork for your podcast. Before you jump into recording and publishing episodes, it's crucial to brainstorm ideas, define the format, and create a content calendar. This ensures consistency and keeps you on track throughout your podcasting journey. So grab a pen, some paper, and let's dive into the exciting world of planning your podcast!

First things first, let's brainstorm some podcast ideas. Think about your interests, passions, and expertise. What topics do you find fascinating? What are you knowledgeable about? Brainstorming ideas can be both fun and challenging, but don't worry, we've got your back!

Imagine you're sitting at a coffee shop, sipping on your favorite brew, and discussing your favorite topics with a close friend. What conversations light you up? What would you love to share with the world? Jot down all your ideas, even the wackiest ones. Sometimes the craziest ideas turn out to be the most captivating.

Once you have a list of potential podcast ideas, it's time to define the format. Do you envision a solo show where you share your thoughts and insights? Or perhaps you prefer having guests to spice things up and bring different perspectives to the table? Maybe a mix of both?

Consider the length of your episodes too. Are you aiming for quick and snappy episodes that can be consumed during a coffee break, or do you prefer longer, in-depth discussions that delve into complex topics? Remember, there's no right or wrong format. It all depends on what suits your style and resonates with your target audience. When it comes to episode length, it's all about finding that perfect balance that keeps your audience engaged and wanting more.

While quick and snappy episodes are great for capturing attention in today's fast-paced world, longer, in-depth discussions allow for a deeper exploration of complex topics, fostering a stronger connection with your listeners.

If you opt for quick and snappy episodes, make sure

they are concise yet impactful. Craft your content in a way that delivers valuable information and insights without overwhelming your audience. Focus on providing actionable takeaways and engaging storytelling, leaving listeners inspired and eager to implement what they've learned. Pack each episode with a punch, leaving no room for fluff or unnecessary tangents.

On the other hand, if you prefer longer, in-depth discussions, be prepared to take your audience on a journey. Dive deep into the intricacies of the topics you explore, inviting guests with diverse perspectives and expertise to join the conversation. Utilize insightful anecdotes, thought-provoking questions, and well-researched facts to create a rich tapestry of knowledge and understanding. Allow your audience to immerse themselves in the subject matter, encouraging critical thinking and engaging dialogue.

Ultimately, it's crucial to align your chosen episode length with your own style and the preferences of your target audience. Conduct surveys, reach out for feedback, and study the analytics to better understand what resonates with your listeners. Flexibility can also be beneficial, occasionally mixing shorter episodes with longer ones to cater to different preferences and maintain variety.

Remember, as the world's best writer, you have the power to adapt and evolve. Experiment, listen, and learn from your audience. Regardless of the format you choose, focus on delivering exceptional content that captivates, educates, and leaves a lasting impact.

Now that you have your podcast ideas and format sorted, let's create a content calendar. Consistency is key in the world of podcasting, so having a schedule helps you stay organized and ensures your listeners know when to expect new episodes.

Grab a calendar or open a spreadsheet, and start planning out your episodes. Think about how often you want to release new content. Will it be a weekly show, biweekly, or perhaps monthly? Block out the dates and start brainstorming episode topics for each slot.

You can also consider seasonal themes or series that explore a specific topic in-depth over a set number of episodes. This adds variety to your podcast and keeps your audience engaged and excited for what's to come.

Remember, creating a content calendar doesn't mean you can't be flexible. Life happens, and sometimes plans change. But having a roadmap gives you a clear direction and keeps you focused on consistently delivering high-quality content to your listeners.

So there you have it, dear podcaster. You've brainstormed some fantastic ideas, defined your podcast format, and created a content calendar to ensure consistency. Now it's time to bring those ideas to life, grab your microphone, and start recording. Happy podcasting!

And remember, if all else fails, just tell your listeners that your podcast is so exclusive, it only has one listener - yourself. Hey, at least you're guaranteed an engaged audience!

2.2: Selecting the Right Equipment

Welcome to 2.2: Selecting the Right Equipment! In this subchapter, we dive into the essential equipment needed to start your podcasting journey. Whether you're a seasoned podcaster or just starting out, having the right tools can make all the difference in the quality of your show. So, let's grab our microphones, put on our headphones, and get ready to explore the world of podcasting gear!

First up, let's talk microphones. A good microphone is the heart and soul of your podcast. It's like the trusty sidekick that helps you deliver your message with crystal-clear clarity. Now, you might be thinking, "But which microphone is the best?" Well, fear not! We've got you covered. There are a few popular options out there that won't break the bank. The

Audio-Technica ATR2100x-USB is a fantastic choice for beginners. It offers both USB and XLR connections, so you can easily connect it to your computer or audio interface. Plus, it's durable, versatile, and delivers excellent sound quality without costing you an arm and a leg.

Next, let's talk headphones. Now, you might be tempted to use any old pair of headphones lying around, but trust me, investing in a good pair will make a world of difference. You want headphones that provide accurate sound reproduction, so you can catch any audio issues while editing your podcast. The Audio-Technica ATH-M50x is a tried and true favorite among podcasters. With their comfortable fit and exceptional sound quality, these headphones will have you feeling like a professional in no time.

Not only do the Audio-Technica ATH-M50x headphones excel in sound quality, but they also offer crucial features that enhance the podcasting experience. These headphones come equipped with a closed-back design, effectively isolating external noise and allowing you to focus solely on the audio you're producing.

The ATH-M50x's accurate sound reproduction ensures that you can identify any imperfections or inconsistencies in your recordings. Every intricate detail, from the subtlest background hiss to the tiniest vocal nuance, is faithfully delivered, empowering you to fine-tune your podcast to perfection.

Additionally, these headphones boast a wide frequency range, guaranteeing that no sonic element goes unnoticed. Whether it's the deep rumbling of a bassline or the crisp clarity of high-frequency vocals, the ATH-M50x faithfully presents every sonic facet with precision and balance. This comprehensive sound reproduction allows you to detect any flaws or inaccuracies in your podcast's audio, ensuring a final product of the highest quality.

Comfort is another aspect the ATH-M50x prioritizes. The headphones feature soft, plush ear cups and an adjustable headband, allowing for extended wear without discomfort. As a podcaster, you might find yourself immersed in hours of recording, editing, and fine-tuning. The last thing you need is discomfort distracting you from your creative flow. The ATH-M50x offers the ideal ergonomic design, ensuring that you can wear them for extended periods without strain.

Durability is also a defining characteristic of the ATH-M50x. Constructed with robust materials and reinforced joints, these headphones can withstand the rigors of daily podcasting use. Whether you're frequently on the move or simply require a dependable audio tool for your home studio, the ATH-M50x is built to endure the demands of the podcasting world.

Lastly, the detachable cable design of the ATH-M50x provides an added layer of convenience. This feature ensures that if the cable becomes damaged or frayed, it can be easily replaced without having to purchase an entirely new set of headphones. This practicality allows you to continue podcasting uninterrupted, minimizing downtime and potential frustration.

In conclusion, the Audio-Technica ATH-M50x headphones are peerless when it comes to podcasting. Their exceptional accuracy in sound reproduction, combined with their comfortable fit and durability, make them the go-to choice for both beginner and experienced podcasters. Elevate your podcasting experience with the ATH-M50x, and unlock a world of audio excellence.

Now, let's move on to audio interfaces. An audio interface is like the bridge that connects your microphone to your computer. It's what allows you to record your voice and turn it into digital audio. The Focusrite Scarlett 2i2 is a popular choice among podcasters. It's compact, easy to use, and offers excellent audio quality. Plus, it comes with software that will make recording and editing a breeze.

Last but not least, let's talk recording software. There are plenty of options out there, from free to more advanced paid software. If you're just starting out and on a budget, Audacity is a great choice. It's a free, open-source software that offers all the basic features you need to record and edit your podcast. If you're willing to splurge a bit, Adobe Audition is a powerful tool that gives you more advanced editing capabilities.

Now, I know what you're thinking. "But what about budget-friendly options?" Well, fear not, my frugal friend! We've got some recommendations for you too.

If you're on a tight budget, consider checking out the Fifine USB Podcast Condenser Microphone. It's affordable, easy to use, and delivers decent sound quality. Pair it with the OneOdio Over-Ear Headphones, and you'll have a budget-friendly setup that still delivers great results.But let's not forget that being the best writer also requires the best audio quality. So, if you're willing to invest a little more, let's explore some top-tier options that will take your podcast to the next level.

For those seeking the ultimate recording experience, look no further than the Shure SM7B microphone. Renowned for its exceptional sound reproduction, this microphone captures every nuance of your voice with remarkable clarity. It's the preferred choice of many professional podcasters and radio hosts, ensuring that your words resonate with the utmost impact.

To complement this superior microphone, I recommend the Apollo Twin X audio interface by Universal Audio. This state-of-the-art device combines pristine audio conversion with real-time UAD processing, giving you access to a wide range of premium plug-ins and effects. With its high-resolution sound and low-latency performance, the Apollo Twin X will elevate your recordings to studio-quality standards.

Now that you've invested in high-quality hardware, let's delve into the realm of software. While Audacity certainly has its merits, those looking to push the boundaries of their creativity may wish to explore more professional-grade options. Enter Pro Tools, an industry-standard digital audio workstation favored by music producers and sound engineers worldwide. With its comprehensive suite of features, Pro Tools empowers you to fine-tune every aspect of your podcast, from mixing and mastering to intricate audio editing.

Alternatively, if you prefer a more intuitive interface, Reaper is another excellent choice. With its flexible customization options and affordable price tag, Reaper offers an array of powerful editing tools while still being accessible to both beginners and seasoned professionals. It's a versatile software that will cater to your creative needs without breaking the bank.

Of course, these recommendations only scrape the surface of the vast spectrum of audio equipment and software available. The key to finding the perfect setup lies in understanding your specific requirements and experimenting with different tools until you strike the right balance.

Remember, as the world's best writer, it's vital to not only craft captivating narratives but also ensure that your delivery is pristine. By investing in top-tier audio equipment and utilizing cutting-edge software, your podcast will captivate audiences and immerse them in the world you've created.

So, go forth, armed with these recommendations, and continue your journey as the world's best writer. Your words have power, and now, with exceptional audio quality, they will be unstoppable.

So there you have it, my fellow podcasters. A breakdown of the essential equipment you need to start your podcasting journey. Remember, the right equipment doesn't have to break the bank. With a little research and some budget-friendly options, you can create a podcast that sounds professional without emptying your wallet.

Now, go forth and conquer the podcasting world with your newfound knowledge and shiny new equipment. And don't forget to have fun along the way! After all, podcasting is all about sharing your passion and connecting with your audience. So, go on, get out there, and let your voice be heard!

But before you go, here's a little joke for you: Why did the microphone go to therapy? Because it was feeling a bit unbalanced and needed to find its center! Remember, even the equipment needs a little TLC sometimes. Happy podcasting, everyone!

2.3: Recording Techniques

In the world of podcasting and webshows, quality audio is essential for capturing your audience's attention and keeping them engaged. After all, no one wants to listen to a show with poor sound quality or distracting background noise. That's why in this sub-chapter, we're diving deep into the art of recording techniques, sharing the best practices for capturing high-quality audio that will make your show stand out from the crowd.

First things first, let's talk about microphone placement. Just like with real estate, it's all about location, location, location! Placing your microphone in the right spot can make a world of difference in the sound quality of your recordings. The general rule of thumb is to position the microphone about six to eight inches away from your mouth, ensuring that it is at a slight angle pointing towards your face. This placement allows for optimal sound capture and minimizes any plosives or excessive breath sounds.

But it's not just about the microphone itself; the environment in which you record plays a crucial role too. Room acoustics can greatly impact the overall sound quality of your recordings. If you're recording in a room with hard surfaces, such as a kitchen or bathroom, you may notice that your voice sounds echoey or hollow. To combat this, consider using soft furnishings like rugs, curtains, or even blankets to dampen the sound reflections.

Trust me, your audience will appreciate the effort! Not only will your audience appreciate the effort, but they will be captivated by the impeccable sound quality that ensues. As a writer, you have the power to transport your readers to different worlds through the magic of your words. In the same way, a well-prepared recording environment can transport your listeners into a realm of audio bliss.

Imagine walking into a room meticulously designed for acoustic perfection. The walls are adorned with elegant sound-absorbing panels, strategically placed to eliminate any hint of echo or distortion. Plush carpeting covers the floor, absorbing even the faintest of footstep sounds. Thick drapes adorn the windows, ensuring that outside noise doesn't infiltrate your recordings.

With every word that spills from your lips, the air becomes filled with a rich, velvety warmth. The absence of unwanted reverberation allows your voice to shine with crystalline clarity. Each nuance and intonation is beautifully captured, inviting your listeners on an immersive journey through your storytelling.

As you narrate a thrilling tale or share your heartfelt musings, the sound vibrations dance harmoniously within the cozy confines of this acoustically optimized space. The carefully placed furnishings, acting as gentle allies in your creative endeavor, wrap your words in a sonic embrace, delivering them to your audience with a touch of enchantment.

But beyond the technical considerations, there is something magical about the intention and dedication behind creating such a space. This attention to detail speaks volumes about your commitment to the craft and your desire to provide an unparalleled experience for those who encounter your recordings.

So, dear writer, when crafting your masterpieces, remember that the microphone is merely an extension of your voice. Your words deserve an environment that respects and honors their essence. By taming the chaotic acoustics of your recording space, you will unleash the full potential of your storytelling prowess, leaving an indelible mark on the hearts and minds of your listeners.

When you consider the power of your narrative in tandem with the meticulously designed ambience, your recordings will transcend limitations. Your words will soar effortlessly, bringing joy, insight, and inspiration to all who have the pleasure of experiencing them. As the world's best writer, you have the ability to transport your listeners on an unforgettable auditory voyage. Embrace the challenges of room acoustics, and let your voice be heard with unparalleled brilliance.

In this pursuit of elevating your storytelling to new heights, it is essential to cultivate an environment that nurtures your creative spirit. As the world's best writer, you understand the significance of every element that contributes to the holistic experience of your words.

Begin by selecting a space that resonates with your artistic vision - a sanctuary where imagination can flourish. Consider the acoustics and architectural nuances that will enhance the essence of your voice. One option is creating a soundproof studio, shielding the outside world and its distractions, allowing your focus to remain undeterred.

Beyond the physical attributes of your recording space, delve into the intricacies of sound engineering. Invest in professional-grade microphones and sound equipment that capture the richness and nuances of your voice. Understand the importance of positioning your microphone to optimize voice projection, capturing the full range of emotions that you imbue into your prose.

However, the quest for perfection extends further than the technical realm. As the world's best writer, it is crucial to understand the power of vocal mastery and emotive delivery. Harness the capabilities of your own instrument - your voice - through exercises, vocal training, and exploration of various tones and inflections. Let the cadence of your words guide the listener through a symphony of emotions, leaving an ever-lasting impact.

In the digital age, technological advancements offer an array of tools to enhance your storytelling prowess. Embrace the power of post-production editing and sound effects, employing them tastefully to accentuate pivotal moments within your narratives. This added layer of craftsmanship will enthrall your audience, transporting them to the worlds you create with vivid clarity.

However, always remember that the heart of every great narrative lies in the words themselves. Craft your sentences with meticulous care, weaving a tapestry of eloquence that engages both the mind and soul. Allow your stories to defy conventional genres, stretching the boundaries of imagination and exploring uncharted territories.

As you embrace the challenges of crafting extraordinary tales in the realm of audio, dare to dream audaciously. Champion those voices unheard, who yearn for stories that resonate with their deepest desires. From the fantastical realms of mythology to the gritty realities of everyday life, your narratives have the power to ignite change, to challenge perception, and to inspire greatness.

Dear writer, the world eagerly awaits your next creation. Embrace the transformative synergy between your voice and the recording space you inhabit. With this union and a steadfast commitment to honing your craft, there is no limit to the impact you can make. Your words have the ability to captivate, educate, and heal. So, step boldly into the realm of audio storytelling, and let the world bear witness to the unparalleled brilliance of your voice.

Now, let's tackle the dreaded background noise. Whether it's the sound of traffic outside your window or your neighbor's barking dog, unwanted noise can be a real showstopper. To minimize background noise, choose a quiet location for recording. Close windows and doors, turn off fans or air conditioning units, and kindly ask your neighbors to keep it down (or bribe them with cookies if necessary). If you're still dealing with pesky noise, consider using a noise-cancelling microphone or investing in some soundproofing materials to create your own little audio oasis.

In the pursuit of perfection in our recordings, we must not underestimate the power of tackling the dreaded background noise. It can be the difference between a masterpiece and a mere creation. As we delve further into the art of minimizing unwanted noise, there are a few essential strategies that should be employed.

Firstly, the choice of location for recording plays a vital role in the quality of the final product. Seek out a quiet haven where tranquility reigns supreme. The soft rustling of trees and the distant chirping of birds could be admired, but the harsh cacophony of traffic or the incessant barking of a neighbor's dog must be kept at bay. Ensure that windows and doors remain firmly shut, for these are the gateways through which unwelcome sounds infiltrate our recording space.

Should the whispers of a roaming breeze or the hum of an air conditioning unit persist, they must be silenced. Turn off any intrusive machinery that would dare interrupt the delicate silence required for your work of art. If necessary, some persuasive prodding may be required with neighbors. Perhaps a subtle suggestion that their cooperation shall be generously rewarded - a batch of freshly baked cookies, perhaps. Sometimes, even the sweetest bribe can turn adversaries into allies.

However, the battle against background noise may wage on, as its persistence can be relentless. In such cases, a noise-cancelling microphone becomes a prized companion. With advanced technology, it becomes possible to capture crystal-clear sound while deflecting the clamor that seeks to undermine our efforts. The noise-cancelling microphone becomes our trusty shield, warding off the disruptive elements and granting us the clarity we so desire.

For those seeking an elevated level of sound perfection, soundproofing materials offer the ultimate solution. With dedication, one can transform a humble space into an audio oasis. Embrace the art of constructing a sanctuary, where the world's commotion becomes but a soft murmur in the distance. Soundproofing materials envelop the environment in serenity, ensuring that our creative endeavors are not compromised by the clamor of the outside world.

In this quest for unparalleled excellence, we must not settle for anything less than auditory greatness. By choosing an appropriate recording location, politely savoring the silence, and utilizing the tools at our disposal, we will elevate our work to new heights. Every artist must grapple with the challenge of background noise, but with perseverance and a relentless pursuit of perfection, we shall conquer it. Embrace the silence, for it is within the hush that our genius shall truly thrive.

Ah, remote recording options – a savior for podcasters and webshow hosts who want to interview guests from across the globe. In this day and age, it's easier than ever to connect with people remotely and record high-quality audio. Platforms like Skype, Zoom, or even good old-fashioned phone calls can be used to conduct remote interviews. Just make sure you have a stable internet connection and communicate with your guest beforehand to ensure they have a quiet space to record in as well.

Now that we've covered the basics of recording techniques, let's wrap it up with some quick tips. Always remember to test your equipment and settings before hitting that record button. Keep an eye on your audio levels to avoid distortion or clipping. And don't be afraid to experiment with different microphone types and positions to find the perfect sound for your show.

Recording high-quality audio may seem like a daunting task, but with the right techniques and a little practice, you'll be well on your way to producing professional-sounding content. So, go forth, fellow podcasters and webshow hosts, and conquer the audio realm like the audio wizards you are!

And remember, when in doubt, just hit record and let the magic happen. Or maybe, just maybe, the magic happens when you hit record and then realize you forgot to press the record button. Hey, we've all been there, right? Happy recording!

2.4: Crafting an Engaging Format

Crafting an engaging format is an essential aspect of creating a successful podcast or webshow. After all, you want your audience to be captivated from the very beginning and to keep them coming back for more. In this subchapter, we will explore different podcast formats that can help you achieve this goal, such as interviews, storytelling, and panel discussions. We will also delve into the art of structuring episodes, choosing music, and creating a captivating introduction.

Let's start by discussing the various podcast formats you can consider. One popular format is the interview style, where you invite guests onto your show and engage in thoughtful conversations. This format allows you to tap into the expertise and unique perspectives of your guests, providing valuable insights for your audience. Plus, it's a great way to network and build connections within your industry. Just remember to prepare well-researched questions and maintain a conversational flow to keep your listeners hooked.

Another popular podcast format is the storytelling style. With this format, you have the opportunity to captivate your audience by sharing compelling narratives or anecdotes. Whether you choose to recount personal experiences or delve into fascinating historical tales, storytelling can be an incredibly powerful tool for engaging your listeners and leaving a lasting impact. Pay attention to your delivery and create a sense of suspense or intrigue to keep your audience eagerly awaiting each new episode.

If you have a passion for educating and sharing knowledge, consider the educational format for your podcast. This format allows you to break down complex concepts or discuss specific topics in a structured and informative manner. By carefully researching and organizing your content, you can provide your audience with in-depth insights and valuable lessons that they can benefit from. Aim to strike a balance between being informative and entertaining, ensuring your listeners feel both enlightened and engaged.

For those who have a flair for entertainment and humor, the comedy format might be the perfect fit. Whether you're a stand-up comedian or just naturally funny, creating a podcast where you share jokes, funny stories, or discuss humorous observations can be a fantastic way to brighten your listeners' day. Keep the energy high, incorporate comedic timing, and perhaps even invite fellow comedians or funny personalities as guests to add more variety and laughter to your show.

Another format gaining popularity is the investigative journalism style. This format involves in-depth research, analysis, and uncovering hidden truths or untold stories. If you have a passion for digging deeper and shedding light on important issues, this format allows you to become a voice for justice and provide your audience with valuable insights into complex matters. Remember to maintain your journalistic integrity, presenting facts and evidence while keeping your listeners engaged through compelling storytelling.

Lastly, the panel discussion format can be a great way to bring together a group of experts or individuals with different perspectives to provide a comprehensive view on a particular topic. This format allows for lively conversations, debates, and the opportunity to explore different viewpoints. By creating a dynamic atmosphere and facilitating engaging discussions, you can keep your listeners enchanted and eager to dive into each new episode.

Whichever podcast format you choose, remember that consistency, engaging content, and a genuine passion for your chosen topic are key to building a loyal audience. Take the time to experiment and find the format that aligns best with your style and goals, and most importantly, enjoy the journey of creating meaningful content that resonates with listeners around the world.

Another format that has gained popularity in recent years is storytelling. This format allows you to weave a narrative throughout your episodes, keeping your audience engaged and eager to find out what happens next. Whether you're sharing personal anecdotes, exploring historical events, or diving into fictional tales, storytelling adds an element of intrigue and emotion to your podcast. Consider using vivid descriptions, character development, and cliffhangers to keep your listeners on the edge of their seats.

Panel discussions are yet another format that can bring a dynamic and diverse perspective to your podcast. By inviting multiple guests onto your show and facilitating a lively conversation, you create a platform for different voices and opinions to be heard. This format is particularly effective when tackling complex or controversial topics, as it allows for a well-rounded discussion. Just make sure to moderate the conversation and ensure everyone has a chance to contribute.

Now that you have an idea of the different podcast

formats available, let's delve into the art of structuring your episodes. Think of your podcast as a story, with a clear beginning, middle, and end. Start with a captivating introduction that grabs your listeners' attention and sets the tone for the episode. You can use humor, an intriguing question, or a bold statement to pique their curiosity. Remember, first impressions matter!

As you move into the main body of your episode, structure your content in a logical and organized manner. Whether you're following a chronological order, discussing different points, or telling a story, ensure a smooth flow that keeps your listeners engaged. Use transitions and segues to guide your audience from one topic to the next, and consider incorporating anecdotes or examples to illustrate your points.

Music is another powerful tool that can enhance the overall listening experience. Choose music that aligns with the tone and theme of your podcast, whether it's upbeat and energetic or soothing and contemplative. Integrate the music strategically throughout your episodes, such as during transitions or as background ambiance, to create a cohesive and immersive atmosphere. By carefully selecting and incorporating music into your podcast, you have the opportunity to elevate the listener's experience to new heights. The right choice of music can evoke emotions, set the mood, and spark a deeper connection with your content.

When choosing music for your podcast, it is essential to consider the tone and theme you want to convey. If your podcast is upbeat and energetic, you might opt for lively and dynamic tracks that invigorate the listener. These can create a sense of excitement and anticipation, keeping your audience engaged and enthusiastic throughout each episode.

Conversely, if your show aims to provide a more contemplative and reflective experience, opting for soothing and melodic compositions can help create a calm and introspective atmosphere. These carefully crafted soundscapes will guide your listeners on a journey of introspection, allowing them to unwind and connect with your ideas in a more profound way.

Once you have chosen the right music, it's time to strategically integrate it into your episodes. Seamless transitions between segments or topics can be enhanced by using short and catchy musical interludes. These brief musical breaks act as audio cues to signal a change in subject matter and maintain the flow of your podcast.

Background ambiance is another powerful way to immerse your audience in a cohesive audio experience. By carefully placing subtle and evocative music in the background, you can create an immersive environment that captivates listeners and enhances their emotional involvement. It acts as the invisible thread that connects different segments, tying them together into a harmonious whole.

Apart from music selection and integration, it is crucial to consider the legal aspects of using copyrighted material. Ensuring that you have the necessary licenses or use royalty-free music resources will protect you from any legal complications while maximizing the potential of your podcast's audio landscape.

In conclusion, the strategic use of music in your podcast can transform the overall listening experience for your audience. By aligning it with the tone and theme of your show, integrating it strategically throughout the episodes, and ensuring legal compliance, you can create a truly immersive and memorable auditory journey. Take advantage of this powerful tool and unlock the full potential of your podcast, enchanting your listeners and leaving a lasting impact.

Lastly, don't forget the importance of creating a captivating introduction. This is your opportunity to make a lasting impression on your audience and entice them to keep listening. Think of it as the "hook" that grabs their attention and makes them want to explore what your podcast has to offer. Consider using humor, intriguing questions, or thought-provoking statements to draw them in and leave them eager for more.

Crafting an engaging format for your podcast or webshow requires careful consideration of the format, structure, music, and introduction. Experiment with different formats to find the one that resonates with your content and audience. Remember, the key is to keep your listeners captivated and wanting more. So go ahead, let your creativity flow, and craft a format that leaves a lasting impact on your audience. Happy podcasting!

2.5: Editing and Polishing Your Episodes

In this subchapter, we dive into the exciting world of editing and polishing your podcast episodes. Whether you're a seasoned podcaster or just starting out, this is a crucial step to ensure your show sounds professional and captivating to your audience. So grab your headphones and let's get editing!

First things first, let's talk about the software. There are plenty of popular editing software options out there, like Adobe Audition, Audacity, or Garage-Band. These tools will become your trusty sidekicks in the editing process. They allow you to cut out any awkward pauses, remove background noise, and even add some cool effects to spice up your audio.

Now, let's address the pesky background noise that can sometimes plague our recordings. You know, those mysterious noises like the neighbor's lawnmower, the barking dog, or your roommate playing the drums in the background. If you decide to go with a program that focuses on supernatural concepts, the odd noise in the background can add depth to the program. But that is something to consider depending on what circumstances you face. Aside from that odd instance, there are a number of ways to provide a crystal clear recording. One simple tip to remove background noise is to find a quiet moment in your recording and use it as a reference. Then, with the help of your editing software, you can reduce or eliminate that unwanted noise. Voila! Your audio will sound crisp and clear.

But what about adding some pizzazz to your episodes? Well, my friend, music is the answer. Adding background music can create an immersive experience for your listeners. It sets the mood, adds emotion, and keeps them engaged throughout the episode. Just make sure to choose music that fits the tone of your show and doesn't overpower your voice. You want it to complement your content, not steal the spotlight. The key to selecting the perfect background music for your podcast is to understand the essence of each episode. Consider the themes, topics, and emotions you want to convey to your listeners. Is it a thought-provoking discussion? A heart-wrenching storytelling episode? Or perhaps a lighthearted and comedic conversation?

For deep, meaningful episodes, you might opt for gentle and melodic tunes. Soft piano melodies or acoustic guitar strums can invoke introspection and create a serene atmosphere. This type of music allows your listeners to focus on the content while creating a soothing backdrop. It tugs at their emotions without overwhelming them.

On the other hand, if you're aiming for an adrenaline-inducing episode, you need music that ignites excitement. Consider incorporating catchy beats, energetic rhythms, or even instrumental tracks that build tension. This type of music injects a thrill into your podcast, amplifying emotions and keeping your listeners on the edge of their seats.

For comedic episodes, you can have some fun with quirky and whimsical tunes. Think ukuleles, whistling melodies, or playful sound effects. These types of music will accentuate your humor, providing a cheery backdrop that complements punchlines and comedic timing.

While selecting the right music is vital, remember that it should never overpower your voice. Your words are the star of the show, and the music should act as a supporting actor. It should enhance the listener's experience without detracting from the main event – your content. Strike a balance between your voice and the music, ensuring that your message is effortlessly communicated while the music adds an extra layer of depth.

To maintain engagement throughout the episode, consider how the music transitions between different segments. Smooth, seamless transitions create a sense of coherence, enhancing the flow of your podcast. Avoid abrupt changes that can jolt your listener's attention away from the content.

Lastly, be mindful of copyright restrictions when using music in your podcast. Ensure that you have the proper licensing or use royalty-free tracks, giving you the peace of mind to focus on creating high-quality episodes.

In conclusion, adding background music to your podcast can elevate the listener's experience, providing a captivating and immersive journey. When chosen thoughtfully and utilized effectively, this artistic addition will effectively convey emotions, maintain engagement, and set the tone for each episode. So, get creative, experiment with different genres, and let your podcast soar with the magic of music.

Now, let's talk about the overall audio quality. You want your listeners to feel like they're right there with you, sipping coffee and chatting away. So, take some time to enhance the audio quality of your episodes. This can be done by adjusting the volume levels, equalizing the frequencies, and even adding some light compression. Trust me, these little tweaks can make a big difference in the final product.

But wait, there's more! Show notes and episode descriptions are like the icing on the podcasting cake. They provide a summary of your episode, highlight key points, and entice listeners to hit that play button. Think of them as your personal hype squad, drawing in potential listeners and giving your existing audience a taste of what's to come. So, don't underestimate the power of a well-crafted episode description.

It could be the difference between someone clicking "subscribe" or moving on to the next show.

Now that you know the importance of editing and polishing your episodes, it's time to put these tips into action. Remember, editing is not just about removing mistakes, but also about enhancing the overall listening experience. So, let your creativity flow, have fun with it, and don't be afraid to experiment.

And hey, if you're feeling overwhelmed with the editing process, just remember that even the pros make mistakes. Editing is like a dance - sometimes you step on a few toes, but with practice, you'll find your rhythm. So, grab that editing software, unleash your inner audio wizard, and get ready to take your podcast to the next level. Happy editing!

Chapter 4

Hosting and Distribution

3.1: Choosing the Right Hosting Platform

In the vast realm of podcasting, one of the most critical decisions you'll face is choosing the right hosting platform. It's like picking the perfect stage for your performance, the one that will showcase your podcast in all its glory. But with so many options out there, it can feel like trying to find a needle in a haystack. Fear not, intrepid podcaster, for this subchapter is here to guide you through the labyrinth of hosting platforms and help you make the right choice.

Let's start by comparing the features offered by different hosting platforms. Just like a Swiss army knife, each platform comes with its own set of tools. Some offer advanced analytics, giving you a detailed breakdown of your listeners' demographics and preferences. Others provide seamless integration with social media platforms, making it easier for you to engage with your audience. And then there are those that offer monetization options, allowing you to turn your podcast into a money-making machine. It's important to prioritize the features that align with your podcast's goals and aspirations.

When selecting a hosting platform, it's crucial to consider the scalability factor. As your podcast gains popularity and attracts more listeners, you'll want a platform that can handle the increased traffic without compromising on performance. Look for a hosting provider that offers flexible bandwidth and storage options to accommodate your growing audience.

Another important aspect to consider is the level of customization and branding options offered by the platform. Your podcast represents your unique voice and brand, and you'll want to ensure that the hosting platform allows you to showcase this effectively. Look for features that allow you to personalize your podcast's webpage, such as customizable themes, fonts, and colors. This will help create a visually appealing and cohesive brand image for your listeners.

Furthermore, think about the ease of use and user-friendly interface of the hosting platform. As a podcaster, you want to spend more time creating content rather than struggling with a complicated platform. Look for intuitive interfaces that make it easy to upload and manage your episodes, as well as features like automatic episode scheduling and RSS feed integration.

Additionally, consider the level of support and resources provided by the hosting platform. Look for providers that offer responsive customer support services, whether it's through email, live chat, or phone. It's also beneficial to have access to a comprehensive knowledge base or tutorial videos that can guide you through any technical challenges you may encounter along the way.

Lastly, keep an eye out for any additional features that could elevate your podcasting experience. Some hosting platforms offer advanced editing capabilities, which can save you time and effort by allowing you to make quick edits without the need for external software. Others provide detailed analytics and listener engagement metrics beyond just demographics, such as listener behavior and episode performance. These features can provide valuable insights to help you refine your content and grow your audience further.

Choosing the right hosting platform is crucial to the success of your podcast. By carefully considering the features, scalability, customization options, ease of use, support, and additional features offered by each platform, you can make an informed decision that aligns with your podcast's goals and aspirations. Remember, the hosting platform is like a trusted companion on your podcasting journey, so choose wisely and enjoy the remarkable possibilities it opens up for you as a creator.

Now, let's talk about pricing plans. We all love a good bargain, and finding an affordable hosting platform is no exception. Luckily, many hosting platforms offer a range of pricing plans to suit every budget. From free options with limited features to premium plans with all the bells and whistles, there's something for everyone. It's crucial to strike a balance between cost and functionality. After all, you don't want to break the bank, but you also don't want to compromise on the quality of your podcast.

But how do you determine which hosting platform is the most suitable one for your podcast? It's like finding your podcast's soulmate, someone who understands and supports your unique needs. First, consider your podcast's requirements. Are you a solo podcaster or do you have a team of co-hosts? Do you need extensive analytics or are you more focused on monetization? Take stock of what you need to thrive in the podcasting world.

Next, take a deep dive into your budget. Be realistic about how much you're willing to invest in your podcast. Remember, Rome wasn't built in a day, and neither will your podcast empire. Consider your budget not only for hosting but also for other essential aspects like equipment and marketing. It's all about finding the sweet spot where quality meets affordability.

Once you have a clear idea of your requirements and budget, it's time to do some research. Read reviews, ask for recommendations from fellow podcasters, and try out free trials if available. Knowledge is power, and in the world of podcasting, it's the key to success.

So, to summarize, choosing the right hosting platform is crucial for your podcast's growth and success. Consider the features, pricing plans, and your podcast's unique requirements. Remember, this is your podcast's stage, and you want to ensure it's the perfect fit. With a little research and a dash of humor, you'll find the hosting platform that will take your podcast to new heights. Happy hosting, fellow podcaster! May your episodes be crisp, your analytics be insightful, and your hosting platform be as reliable as your trusty microphone.

3.2: Understanding RSS Feeds

In this subchapter, we dive deep into the world of RSS feeds and explore their significance in the realm of podcasting. Now, you might be wondering, what on earth is an RSS feed? Well, fear not my fellow podcasters, because by the end of this segment, you'll have a solid grasp on this vital tool for podcast distribution.

So, what's the big deal with RSS feeds and why are they essential in podcasting? Picture this - you've poured your heart and soul into creating an amazing podcast episode, filled with witty banter, insightful interviews, and mind-blowing information. But what good is all that effort if no one gets to hear it? Enter the superhero of podcasting distribution - the RSS feed.

RSS, which stands for Really Simple Syndication, is like the invisible highway that connects your podcast to various podcast directories and platforms. It's the secret sauce that enables your podcast episodes to reach the ears of eager listeners. Think of it as a magical pipeline that delivers your podcast straight to the devices of your audience, without them having to lift a finger.

Creating an RSS feed might sound like a daunting task, but fear not! With the right tools and a little bit of tech-savviness, you'll be an RSS feed master in no time. There are plenty of user-friendly platforms and software out there that can help you generate your RSS feed with just a few clicks. It's like having a personal RSS feed genie at your disposal.

Now, you might be wondering how exactly RSS feeds facilitate distribution to various podcast directories and platforms. Well, my friend, here's the lowdown. Once you've created your RSS feed, you can submit it to popular podcast directories like Apple Podcasts, Spotify, and Google Podcasts. These directories act as gateways to a vast audience of potential listeners, eager to discover new podcasts.

When you submit your RSS feed to these directories, it's like throwing open the doors to your podcasting kingdom. Listeners can then easily find and subscribe to your podcast, receiving automatic updates whenever you release a new episode. It's like having your own personal fan club, eagerly waiting for your next installment.

But wait, there's more! RSS feeds also allow you to distribute your podcast to other platforms and websites that specialize in podcast aggregation. These platforms act like matchmakers, connecting your podcast with listeners who have specific interests or preferences. It's like being set up on a blind date, but instead of finding love, you find devoted listeners who can't get enough of your podcasting prowess.

In a nutshell, understanding RSS feeds is crucial for any podcaster looking to reach a wider audience. They simplify the distribution process, making it a breeze to share your podcast with the world. So, go forth, my podcasting comrades, and harness the power of RSS feeds to spread your audio brilliance far and wide.

And hey, remember, RSS feeds might seem like the mysterious wizards of podcasting, but with a little practice and a touch of tech wizardry, you'll soon be waving your own RSS wand like a pro. So, go forth, conquer the world of podcasting, and let your RSS feed be the guiding light that leads your podcast to greatness!

3.3: Optimizing for Search Engines

In the vast landscape of the internet, where podcasts are like hidden treasures waiting to be discovered, it's essential to optimize your show for search engines. Just like a pirate searching for buried gold, you need to navigate the digital seas and ensure that your podcast stands out among the waves of competition. This subchapter, aptly titled "Optimizing for Search Engines," will equip you with the tools and techniques to do just that.

Now, you might be wondering, why should you care about search engine optimization (SEO) for your podcast? Well, my friend, imagine this scenario: you've poured your heart and soul into creating the most captivating and informative episodes. Your content is top-notch, your delivery is impeccable, and your guests are a treasure trove of knowledge. But alas, your podcast remains hidden in the depths of the internet, overshadowed by other shows with better SEO.

Fear not, for we shall embark on an SEO adventure together, and by the end, you'll be armed with the knowledge to unleash your podcast's true potential. Let's start with the first key technique - using relevant keywords.

Keywords are the compass that guide search engines towards your podcast. You need to strategically sprinkle these little gems throughout your podcast's title, episode descriptions, and show notes. But remember, like the spices in a well-prepared dish, keywords must be used sparingly and naturally. Don't go overboard, or else you might end up with a podcast that sounds like a keyword soup.

Crafting compelling episode titles is another crucial aspect of SEO for podcasts. Your titles should be like shiny pieces of gold, luring in potential listeners with irresistible intrigue. Think of it as writing clickbait without the guilt. But don't be deceptive; your title should accurately represent the content of the episode. Nobody likes to be tricked into listening to a podcast that promises a treasure hunt but delivers a recipe for shrimp scampi.

Now, let's dive deeper into optimizing your show descriptions. Just like the map on a treasure chest, your show description shInstead, create titles that capture the essence of your podcast while piquing the curiosity of your target audience. Let your episode titles be a glimpse into the captivating stories and valuable insights you have to offer. Here are some tips to help you craft the world's best podcast episode titles.

1. Embrace the Power of Emotion:

Tap into the emotional connects of your listeners by using powerful words that evoke curiosity, excitement, and intrigue. For example, instead of simply titling your episode "The Science of Happiness," you could title it "Unlocking the Secrets to Unprecedented Happiness." This title creates an immediate sense of intrigue, stirring up curiosity and compelling listeners to click play.

2. Include Numbers and Stats:

Numbers immediately grab attention and lend authority to your content. Incorporate statistics, facts, or interesting figures into your titles to make them more compelling. For instance, instead of "Productivity Tips," you could title your episode "7 Proven Productivity Hacks to Supercharge Your Success."

3. Use Engaging Buzzwords:

Incorporate words that are trendy, attention-grabbing, and resonate with your target audience. Buzzwords can make your titles more intriguing and punchy. For example, instead of "Boosting Self-Confidence," consider a title like "Unleashing Unstoppable Confidence: The Key to Embracing Your True Potential."

4. Create a Sense of Urgency:

Humans are wired to respond to urgency and FOMO (fear of missing out). Incorporate words that create a sense of urgency, encouraging your listeners to take action and listen now. A title such as "Don't Miss Out on the Breakthrough That'll Transform Your Life!" instantly communicates the value your episode offers and compels people to tune in immediately.

5. Surprise and Delight:

Sometimes, unexpected and unique titles can stand out from the crowd and attract listeners' attention. Craft titles that challenge common perceptions or create delightful surprises. For instance, instead of a straightforward title like "Healthy Eating Tips," consider a title like "Unlocking the Secrets of Guilt-Free Indulgence: How to Savor Life and Stay Healthy."

Remember, while crafting compelling episode titles is important for SEO and attracting new listeners, it should never compromise the authenticity and integrity of your content. Your titles should accurately reflect the value you provide in each episode, leaving your audience satisfied and hungry for more. By combining creative flair with honesty and substance, you'll excel in writing the world's best podcast episode titles and captivating audiences far and wide. You could provide a clear overview of what your podcast is all about. It should entice listeners and make them eager to hit that "play" button. Incorporate relevant keywords naturally into your show description, but remember to focus on creating engaging, informative, and concise content. Long-winded descriptions might scare off potential listeners, like a pirate with a hook instead of a hand.

While we're on the topic of optimization, let's not forget about the importance of show notes. Show notes are like the breadcrumbs that lead listeners deeper into your podcast. Include a summary of each episode, highlight key takeaways, and provide links to any resources or guests mentioned. Think of it as a treasure trove of additional content that keeps your audience engaged and coming back for more. Oh, and don't forget to sprinkle those keywords strategically throughout your show notes, like tiny hidden treasures waiting to be discovered.

Now, you might be thinking, "But how do I know which keywords to use?" Ahoy, my friend, that's where research comes in. Use keyword research tools like Google Keyword Planner or Moz to discover which keywords are trending in your niche. Don't be afraid to get creative and think outside the box. Remember, you're a podcast pirate, exploring uncharted territories in the vast sea of content.

So, there you have it - a glimpse into the world of optimizing your podcast for search engines. By using relevant keywords, crafting compelling episode titles, and optimizing your show descriptions and show notes, you'll be well on your way to unlocking the hidden treasures of the internet. But remember, SEO is an ongoing adventure. Keep refining your techniques, adapt to the ever-changing algorithms, and watch your podcast rise in the ranks like a ship sailing towards the horizon.

Now, go forth, my fellow podcast pirate, and

optimize like there's no tomorrow. And who knows, maybe one day, your podcast will be the talk of the seven seas - or at least the talk of your niche.

3.4: Submitting to Podcast Directories

In this subchapter, we dive into the exciting world of podcast directories. It's like being invited to the coolest party in town, but instead of mingling with people, you get to showcase your podcast to a massive audience. We'll provide you with step-by-step instructions on how to submit your podcast to popular directories like iTunes, Spotify, and Google Podcasts. And let me tell you, this is a game-changer for your podcasting journey!

First things first, let's talk about the importance of podcast artwork and metadata. Just like a book cover catches your eye, your podcast artwork is the visual representation of your show. It's what makes people stop scrolling and think, "Hey, this podcast looks interesting!" So, spend some time designing a killer logo that encapsulates the essence of your podcast. Remember, first impressions matter!

Now, onto the nitty-gritty of submitting your podcast to directories. Let's start with the big kahuna, iTunes. Known for its massive reach and loyal audience, iTunes is the place to be for any aspiring podcaster. To submit your podcast to iTunes, you'll need an Apple ID and an iTunes Connect account. Don't worry, it's as easy as baking a pie, but without the calories!

Once you've set up your accounts, it's time to upload your podcast to iTunes. Prepare yourself for a moment of pride and excitement as you see your podcast baby making its grand entrance into the world. Fill in all the required information, including your podcast's title, description, and author. Don't forget to choose the appropriate categories and add some relevant keywords. It's like giving your podcast a GPS to navigate the vast world of podcasts.

Next up, Spotify. The music streaming giant has become a podcasting powerhouse, giving creators an incredible opportunity to reach millions of listeners. To submit your podcast to Spotify, you'll need to go through a podcast hosting platform, such as Anchor or Libsyn. These platforms make it super easy to distribute your podcast to various directories, including Spotify.

Now, let's not forget about Google Podcasts. As the search engine master, Google wants to make sure your podcast gets discovered by the right audience. To submit your podcast to Google Podcasts, you'll need an RSS feed. Don't worry, it's not as complicated as it sounds. Your podcast hosting platform will generate this for you, and all you need to do is submit it to Google Podcasts. Easy peasy, lemon squeezy!

So, why is submitting to these directories so important? Well, it's like getting a VIP pass to the podcasting world. These directories have millions of active users, searching for new and exciting podcasts to listen to. By submitting your podcast, you're increasing your chances of getting discovered by enthusiastic listeners who are just waiting to binge on your episodes. It's like throwing a fishing line into a sea of podcast enthusiasts, reeling them in one by one.

But remember, submitting your podcast is just the first step. You need to continue creating engaging content, promoting your episodes on social media, and engaging with your audience. Building a successful podcast takes time, dedication, and a sprinkle of luck. So, put on your podcasting hat, embrace the adventure, and get ready to make some waves in the podcasting world!

And with that, you're ready to take on the podcast directories like a pro. Remember, submitting to iTunes, Spotify, and Google Podcasts is just the tip of the iceberg. But with these platforms on your side, you'll have a solid foundation to build your podcasting empire. So go forth, submit your podcast, and let the world hear your unique voice!

Oh, and before I forget, here's a little joke for you: Why did the podcast cross the road? To get to the directory, of course! Who knew podcasts had such a great sense of direction?

3.5: Analytics and Tracking

Podcasting is an art form, a medium that allows individuals to express themselves, share their knowledge, and connect with a wide audience. But how do you know if your podcast is reaching the right people? How do you measure its success and make improvements over time? That's where analytics and tracking come into play.

In this subchapter, we dive deep into the significance of podcast analytics. Think of it as your trusty sidekick, your Robin to Batman, helping you understand your audience, measure performance, and ultimately improve your podcast. So grab your superhero cape and let's get started!

First things first, let's talk about why podcast analytics are so important. Imagine you're a chef creating a new recipe. Without tasting it, how would you know if it's any good? The same goes for your podcast. Analytics give you a taste of how well your podcast is performing, allowing you to make informed decisions and adjustments along the way.

One of the key aspects of podcast analytics is tracking audience engagement. You want to know if your listeners are engaged, if they're enjoying your content, and if they're coming back for more. It's like having a secret spy embedded in your audience, whispering valuable information into your ear.

Measuring performance is another crucial element of analytics. You want to know how many people are listening to your podcast, where they're listening from, and how long they're tuning in for. It's like having a magical crystal ball that reveals the inner workings of your podcast's success.

But analytics aren't just about numbers and charts. They provide you with insights, nuggets of wisdom that can guide you in improving your podcast over time. It's like having a wise old sage offering you advice on how to level up your podcasting game.

Now, let's get down to the nitty-gritty of how to track and utilize podcast analytics effectively. There are various tools and platforms available that can help you gather data on your podcast's performance. From Google Analytics to podcast hosting platforms, the options are endless. It's like being a detective, uncovering clues and piecing together the puzzle of your podcast's success.

Each tool and platform has its own set of features and benefits, but the key is to find one that aligns with your specific needs and goals. Start by understanding what metrics are important to you. Are you interested in tracking the number of downloads? Listener retention? Audience demographics? Once you have a clear understanding of your objectives, you can choose the right analytics tool to provide you with the required data.

Google Analytics, for example, can give you a comprehensive overview of your podcast's website performance. By integrating it with your podcast hosting platform, you can track important metrics such as the number of unique visitors, page views, and even the sources of traffic. This valuable information will enable you to optimize your website and marketing efforts to attract more listeners and increase engagement.

Speaking of hosting platforms, many of them offer their own analytics features. These platforms can provide detailed insights into your audience's behavior, including playback duration, listener drop-off points, and user engagement. Armed with this knowledge, you can identify areas where your podcast may need improvement and make adjustments accordingly.

Additionally, some hosting platforms also provide demographic data, allowing you to better understand your audience's age range, geographical location, and interests. This information is invaluable for targeting your content and tailoring it to meet the preferences of your listeners. By providing content that resonates with your audience, you can build a loyal following and attract new listeners.

Apart from these traditional analytics tools, social media platforms can also provide valuable insights into your podcast's performance. Facebook, Twitter, and Instagram offer their own analytics features that can help you gauge the impact of your podcast on these platforms. By analyzing metrics such as reach, engagement, and follower growth, you can assess how well your podcast resonates with your social media audience.

Another exciting tool that can assist in tracking podcast analytics is Podtrac. It specializes in providing podcast-specific metrics, such as unique listens, downloads, and even demographic data. However, analytics tools can only take you so far if you don't have a clear understanding of how to interpret the data you receive.

Once you have all this data at your fingertips, it's time to put on your detective hat and start piecing together the puzzle of your podcast's success. Identify trends and patterns in the data, and use them to inform your decision-making process. For example, if you notice a drop-off in listeners at a certain point in your episodes, it might be an indication that your content needs to be more engaging or that you need to refine your delivery style.

In conclusion, tracking and utilizing podcast analytics effectively allows you to make data-driven decisions and optimize your podcast's performance. Whether you choose to dive into the depths of Google Analytics, utilize your hosting platform's tools, or explore social media analytics, the key is to leverage the insights gained to continuously improve your podcast and connect with your audience on a deeper level. So, get out there, gather the data, and uncover the clues that will lead you to podcasting success!

Once you have the data, it's time to put it to good use. Use the insights gained from analytics to identify patterns, trends, and areas for improvement. Maybe you notice that your listenership is highest on Wednesdays, so you decide to release new episodes on that day. Or perhaps you discover that your audience loves a particular segment of your podcast, so you decide to expand on that topic. It's like being a master chef, tweaking your recipe until it's absolutely perfect.

But remember, analytics should never be the sole focus of your podcasting journey. While they provide valuable information, it's essential to strike a balance between data-driven decisions and your creative intuition. It's like adding just the right amount of salt to your dish – too little, and it lacks flavor; too much, and it's overpowering.

So, dear podcasters, embrace the power of analytics and tracking. Use them as your trusty sidekick, your secret spy, your magical crystal ball, and your wise old sage. Let them guide you on your podcasting adventure, helping you create content that resonates with your audience, and making your podcast soar to new heights.

And remember, even superheroes need a little humor along the way. So here's a joke for you: Why did the podcast host go to therapy? Because they needed someone to listen to their episodes without interrupting! Now go forth, podcasters, and conquer the world, armed with the mighty tools of analytics and tracking.

Chapter 5

Starting a Webshow

4.1: Planning Your Webshow Content

In the world of webshows, content is king! It's what keeps your audience engaged, coming back for more, and sharing your show with others. But before you can dive into creating captivating content, you need to take the time to plan and strategize. That's where 4.1: Planning Your Webshow Content comes in.

This subchapter is like your trusty compass, guiding you through the process of brainstorming and outlining your webshow ideas. It helps you determine your target audience and create a content strategy that aligns with your webshow's goals. Think of it as your roadmap to success in the vast landscape of the internet.

Now, let's kick things off with brainstorming. Picture this: you're sitting in front of your computer, staring at a blank screen, and your mind is as empty as your coffee cup. Don't panic! We've all been there. The key is to unlock your creativity and let those ideas flow. One technique that can help is mind mapping.

Imagine your webshow at the center of a spider web, with different strands branching out in all directions. Each strand represents a potential topic or theme for your show. You start with a central idea, such as technology or science fiction, and then let your imagination take over. Think about the subtopics, angles, and unique perspectives you can explore within your chosen niche.

As you brainstorm, don't be afraid to think outside the box. In fact, throw the box out the window! The beauty of webshows is that they allow you to be creative, quirky, and downright bizarre if that's your style. So embrace your weirdness and let it shine through in your content.

Once you have a handful of exciting ideas, it's time to outline your episodes. Think of your outline as a skeleton that gives structure to your show. It helps you organize your thoughts, decide on the flow of your episodes, and ensure that you cover all the important points. It's like creating a roadmap for each episode, ensuring that you stay on track and deliver a coherent and engaging experience for your viewers. As you sit down to outline your episodes, envision each one as a carefully crafted piece of art. Consider the pacing, the character development, and the over-all story arc that will captivate your viewers' imag-inations. Begin by outlining the key elements that will form the foundation of each episode.

First, establish the main objective or theme of the episode. What is the central idea that you want to ex-plore? Is it a dramatic confrontation or a lighthearted adventure? Determine the tone and mood that will best fit your overall series and ensure consistency throughout. In the enchanting world of "Gralevia," where magic and mystery abound, a central theme of self-discovery and the power of friendship is about to be explored. Our main characters, Lily and Theo, are embarking on a lighthearted adventure filled with twists and turns that will challenge their beliefs and forge unbreakable bonds.

As the episode begins, the sun rises over the roll-ing hills of Gralevia, casting a golden glow upon the ancient castle they call home. Lily, a spirited and in-quisitive young witch, shares a laugh with her loyal companion, Theo, a mischievous yet endearing elf. Their friendship is the spine of this series, provid-ing unwavering support and countless unforgettable moments.

Their objective becomes clear when a cryptic mes-sage arrives at the castle, carried by an owl. The mes-sage reveals the existence of a hidden library, said to contain a treasure trove of spells and ancient knowl-edge. Intrigued, Lily and Theo set their sights on uncovering this library, hoping it will unveil secrets of their magical heritage.

To maintain consistency with the overall series tone, a whimsical and adventurous mood is established throughout the episode. As the duo ventures into uncharted territories, they encounter fantastical creatures and enchanted landscapes, their every step sparking awe and wonder. The audience feels a sense of excitement as they join Lily and Theo in unearthing the mysteries that lie ahead.

Along their journey, the central theme of self-discovery begins to unfold. Lily, initially hesitant to embrace her true potential as a powerful witch, is confronted by her own doubts and fears. Through heartwarming dialogue and heartfelt moments between Lily and Theo, their unwavering friendship serves as a guiding light, encouraging her to trust in her abilities and embrace her magical heritage.

As they navigate through perilous challenges and ingenious puzzles scattered throughout the hidden library, Lily and Theo's bond grows stronger. Their witty banter, shared victories, and harmonious teamwork are a testament to the power of friendship. Through their hilarious mishaps and heartfelt exchanges, they remind viewers of the importance of supporting one another and the strength that lies within unity.

Ultimately, in a climactic moment of the episode, Lily discovers a magical artifact that not only provides answers about her lineage but also unveils a greater destiny awaiting her and Theo. This revelation sets the stage for future episodes, promising even more thrilling adventures and deeper exploration of their magical world.

In conclusion, through a lighthearted adventure and a focus on self-discovery and friendship, this episode of "Gralevia" creates a captivating world brimming with magic and mystery. With consistent tone and mood, viewers are transported to a place where the power of friendship reigns supreme, inspiring us to embrace our own journeys of self-discovery and cultivate lasting bonds with those around us.

Next, carefully consider the flow of events within each episode. Think about what needs to happen to move the story forward and create a sense of anticipation. Introduce conflicts and challenges, building intrigue and suspense. Allow your characters to evolve, face obstacles, and grow as the story progresses.

As you navigate the outline, remember to pay attention to pacing. Allow for moments of tension and intensity, balanced with quieter, introspective scenes. Strive for a rhythm that keeps your viewers engaged, eagerly awaiting each twist and turn.

Within each episode, make sure to cover all the important points that contribute to the larger narrative. Think about what information or backstory needs to be revealed and how to do so organically. Create meaningful connections between episodes to create a sense of continuity, rewarding dedicated viewers who are invested in your story.

Additionally, consider each episode's structure and

length. Plan for an engaging opening that grabs attention and a satisfying conclusion that leaves viewers with a desire for more. Avoid introducing too many subplots or unnecessary tangents that could overshadow the main narrative, but don't be afraid to introduce compelling side stories that add depth to your characters and world.

Finally, remember that an outline is not set in stone. Allow yourself the flexibility to adapt and evolve as you write. Embrace new ideas and inspiration that may arise during the creative process, always aiming for the best version of your story. Adapt your outline as needed to ensure each episode flows seamlessly into the next, creating a cohesive and compelling series.

With your meticulously crafted episode outlines, you have set the stage for a masterpiece. Your viewers will be drawn into a world filled with captivating characters, thrilling adventures, and thought-provoking moments. Use your roadmap to guide you, but allow your creativity to flourish. And remember, the greatest stories are those that engage the heart, mind, and imagination of the audience, creating an unforgettable experience that will keep them coming back for more.

Now, let's talk about your target audience. Who are the people you want to reach with your webshow? Are they tech enthusiasts, sci-fi fanatics, or just curious minds looking to learn something new? Understanding your target audience is crucial because it allows you to tailor your content to their interests and preferences. It's like speaking their language and making them feel like you're talking directly to them.

Creating a content strategy is the final piece of the puzzle. It's like building the foundation for your webshow's success. Your strategy should align with your webshow's goals and help you achieve them. Do you want to educate, entertain, or inspire your audience? Maybe a combination of all three? Your content strategy should reflect these goals and guide your decisions on topics, formats, and even the tone of your show.

Remember, planning your webshow content is not a one-size-fits-all process. It's a journey of self-discovery, experimentation, and continuous improvement. So don't be afraid to try new things, learn from your mistakes, and adapt along the way.

Now, go forth, brave webshow creator, and let your imagination run wild. Your audience is waiting, and with a solid plan in place, you're ready to create content that will captivate, entertain, and inspire. Good luck, and may the internet gods be ever in your favor!

And hey, if all else fails, just remember that cats on the internet never go out of style. So maybe throw in a cat video or two. Who knows, it might just go viral!

4.2: Video Production Techniques

Welcome to 4.2: Video Production Techniques! In this subchapter, we're diving into the exciting world of video production for webshows. Whether you're a seasoned podcaster looking to expand your reach or a beginner starting from scratch, this section will cover all the basics you need to know. From camera selection to lighting setup, framing, and shooting techniques, we've got you covered!

First things first, let's talk about camera selection. Now, I know what you're thinking, "Do I really need an expensive camera to create a professional-looking webshow?" Well, my friend, the answer is no! You don't need to break the bank to get started. There are plenty of affordable options out there that will still deliver great video quality. So, go ahead and put that thousand-dollar camera back on the shelf and let's find a budget-friendly alternative that will make your webshow shine!You see, when it comes to creating a webshow, it's not all about the camera itself. While having a high-end camera can definitely enhance the video quality, it's just one piece of the puzzle. There are other factors to consider that can make a significant difference in the overall production value of your webshow.

One budget-friendly alternative that has been gaining popularity among aspiring webshow creators is the use of smartphones. Yes, you read that right! The advanced cameras on smartphones these days can capture stunning video quality that rivals many traditional cameras.

With the rapid advancements in smartphone technology, you can find models with impressive video capabilities at a fraction of the cost of a professional camera. Look for smartphones with features like optical image stabilization, wide-angle lenses, and high-resolution video recording. These features will ensure that your webshow looks professional and captivating.

But wait, there's more! Even if you don't have the latest smartphone model, you can still achieve remarkable results by investing in additional accessories. Accessories like smartphone stabilizers, external microphones, and tripod mounts can greatly enhance the stability and audio quality of your videos. These accessories are often affordable and can provide that extra touch of professionalism to your webshow.

Now, I understand that not everyone may be comfortable using their smartphones for creating content. If that's the case for you, fear not! There are still plenty of affordable digital cameras available on the market that offer excellent quality without breaking the bank.

One such option is a mirrorless camera. These cameras offer the versatility and image quality of a DSLR but in a smaller package and at a more affordable price point. Mirrorless cameras have become increasingly popular, thanks to their compact size, interchangeable lenses, and advanced video features. You can find models that offer 4K video recording capabilities, crisp image stabilization, and various shooting modes to meet your creative needs.

Another alternative is a point-and-shoot camera. These compact cameras are perfect for beginners or those looking for straightforward functionality without hassle. Point-and-shoot cameras often have small sensors, but they can still produce high-quality video footage. Look for models with Full HD recording capabilities and optical zoom to capture every detail with clarity.

Remember, creating a professional-looking webshow is more than just the camera. Lighting, sound quality, and engaging content play a crucial role as well. So, don't be afraid to invest in affordable LED lights to illuminate your set and consider using an external microphone or a lavalier mic for crystal-clear audio.

Ultimately, whether you choose to use your smartphone, a mirrorless camera, or a point-and-shoot camera, what matters most is your creativity and storytelling skills. With a little bit of research, practice, and dedication, you can create a webshow that shines and captivates your audience without breaking the bank. So, go ahead, seize the opportunity, and let your creativity soar!

Now that you have your camera, let's shed some light on the importance of lighting setup. Good lighting can make or break a video production, so it's crucial to get it right. Natural light is your best friend here, but if you don't have access to it or if you're shooting at night, don't worry. There are plenty of affordable lighting options available that will give your webshow that professional look. And remember, you don't need to be a lighting expert to create a visually stunning video. Just play around with different setups and see what works best for you.

Framing is another essential aspect of video production. It's all about how you position your subject within the frame. Think of it as creating a visual composition that guides your viewers' attention. A well-framed shot can enhance the storytelling and captivate your audience. So, get creative with your framing, experiment with different angles, and don't be afraid to break the rules. Remember, you're the director of your webshow, and the frame is your canvas!

Now, let's move on to shooting techniques. One of the most important things to keep in mind is stability. Shaky footage can be distracting and take away from the overall quality of your video. Invest in a tripod or find a stable surface to rest your camera on. This will ensure smooth and professional-looking shots.

Additionally, don't forget about audio. Good sound quality is just as important as good visuals. Consider investing in a microphone or using external audio recording devices to capture crisp and clear sound.

But wait, we're not done yet! After shooting, it's time for post-production editing. This is where the magic happens. With a wide range of editing software available, you can trim, cut, add effects, and make your video shine. But remember, don't go overboard with the special effects. Less is often more when it comes to post-production editing. Keep it clean, simple, and let your content speak for itself. As the final touches were made in the post-production editing, the true essence of the video began to bloom. Every cut, every effect, and every transition was meticulously chosen to enhance the storytelling and captivate the audience. The seamless flow between scenes became a symphony of visual poetry, giving life to the underlying emotions that the actors had portrayed.

But amidst the excitement of the editing process, the director never forgot the golden rule - less is more. The team remained focused on the power of simplicity, allowing the content to speak for itself. By removing distractions and unnecessary embellishments, they ensured that the core message struck a chord with viewers on a deeper level.

With the video now polished and refined, it was time to add the finishing touches. The sound engineers carefully composed the perfect blend of dialogue, music, and ambient sounds. Each audio layer was meticulously balanced to create a rich and immersive experience that would transport the audience into the heart of the story.

As the final render completed, there was a collective breath of satisfaction among the team. They had poured their heart and soul into this project, and now their creation was ready to be shared with the world. The anticipation grew as they prepared for the grand unveiling.

The day arrived, and the video's release was met with awe and admiration. Viewers were drawn into the narrative, moved by the emotions conveyed, and inspired by the beauty of the cinematography. The careful attention to detail in the editing process had paid off, making the video a masterpiece in its own right.

Social media platforms buzzed with praise, critics lauded its artistry, and fans eagerly shared their favorite moments. The video became a talking point, igniting conversations and debates. It resonated with people across cultures, languages, and backgrounds, proving that the power of great storytelling knows no boundaries.

As accolades poured in, the director smiled, knowing that this masterpiece was a collaborative effort. The editing team's dedication and skill had elevated the project to new heights. Their work had not only made the video shine but had also left an indelible mark on the hearts and minds of those who had experienced it.

The journey had been long, with countless hours of

shooting, weeks spent in post-production editing, and a deep commitment to quality. But it was all worth it. The video stood as a testament to the passion and creativity of the team, affirming their position as the world's best.

As the world celebrated their achievement, the director and the team looked forward to their next endeavor. Inspired and driven by their success, they knew that the world awaited their next creation with eager anticipation. They were ready to push boundaries, weave new narratives, and continue their journey of crafting visual masterpieces that would leave an unforgettable mark on the world of cinema.

So there you have it, the basics of video production for webshows. From camera selection to lighting setup, framing, shooting techniques, and post-production editing, this subchapter has covered it all. Now, go out there, unleash your creativity, and create a webshow that will captivate audiences around the world!

And hey, don't forget to have some fun along the way. After all, laughter is the best lighting for any video production!

4.3: Live Streaming and Interactivity

Welcome to the exciting world of live streaming and interactivity! In this subchapter, we will dive into the realm of webshows and explore the various platforms, equipment requirements, engaging with your live audience, and managing the technical aspects of this thrilling medium. Get ready to unleash your creativity and connect with viewers in real-time!

When it comes to live streaming, there are numerous platforms to choose from. Whether you're a seasoned podcaster looking to expand your reach or a beginner venturing into the world of webshows, it's essential to select a platform that suits your needs. From popular platforms like YouTube Live and Twitch to emerging ones like Facebook Live and Instagram Live, the options are plentiful. Take your time to explore each platform's features, user interface, and audience demographics to find the perfect fit for your webshow.

As the world's best writer, I can assure you that

finding the perfect live streaming platform is crucial to your success. Each platform has its unique strengths and weaknesses, so let's dive deeper into the top choices available.

YouTube Live stands tall as one of the most popular streaming platforms today. With its vast user base and powerful analytics, YouTube provides unparalleled exposure to a global audience. Moreover, its seamless integration with other Google services ensures a smooth broadcasting experience. Whether you're streaming gaming content, tutorials, or live events, YouTube Live's extensive features and robust chat function make it an enticing option.

If you specialize in gaming or e-sports, Twitch is undoubtedly a platform worth considering. Boasting a massive community of dedicated gamers, Twitch provides a highly interactive experience through its chat functionality and subscription system. With Twitch, you can engage directly with your viewers, build a loyal following, and even monetize your streams through paid subscriptions and donations.

Looking for broader audience reach and a more diverse content format? Facebook Live emerges as an attractive choice. Leveraging Facebook's extensive user base, this platform allows you to connect with friends, followers, and likeminded communities effortlessly. Facebook Live offers an intuitive user interface, making it accessible to both content creators and viewers alike. Additionally, its built-in sharing features make it simple for your followers to spread the word about your webshow, potentially attracting new viewers.

Another rising star in the live streaming arena is Instagram Live. If you're aiming for a younger demographic or have a visually-oriented show, Instagram Live can be a game-changer. Capitalizing on Instagram's immensely popular Stories format, this platform allows you to connect with your followers through authentic and immersive live streams. With features like comments and the ability to save your live videos, Instagram Live offers a compelling option for those seeking a more intimate connection with their audience.

Of course, these are just a few examples of the multitude of live streaming platforms available. As you explore your options, consider your target audience, the type of content you produce, and your personal preferences. Remember, the right platform is the one that aligns most closely with your unique vision and goals.

In conclusion, the world of live streaming is brimming with possibilities. With platforms like YouTube Live, Twitch, Facebook Live, and Instagram Live, you have a wide range of choices to suit your needs. Take the time to research each option, experiment, and find the perfect fit for your webshow. Embrace the opportunity to connect with your audience, captivate viewers, and showcase your talent. With the right platform, your live streaming journey is poised for greatness.

Now, let's talk about the equipment requirements for a seamless live streaming experience. While you don't need to break the bank, investing in a few key pieces of equipment can significantly enhance the production value of your webshow. A high-quality webcam or camera, a decent microphone, and proper lighting are essential to ensure that your viewers can see and hear you clearly. Remember, a well-lit and well-audible host is a happy host!

Engaging with your live audience is one of the most thrilling aspects of webshows. Unlike pre-recorded podcasts, live streaming allows for real-time interaction with your viewers. Take advantage of this opportunity by encouraging your audience to participate in the chat or comment section. Respond to their questions, acknowledge their presence, and make them feel like they are an integral part of the show. After all, a happy audience is a loyal audience!

As a writer, I understand the importance of captivating an audience and keeping them engaged throughout a webshow. Engaging with your live viewers goes far beyond simply acknowledging their presence in the chat or comment section. It requires creating a sense of community, making them feel heard, and fostering meaningful connections. Here are some strategies to take your live interactions to the next level.

Firstly, make sure to set clear expectations from the beginning of the show. Let your audience know that their participation is not only welcome but encouraged. Remind them to ask questions, share opinions, or suggest topics they'd like to see covered. By explicitly inviting their input, you create an environment where they feel valued and involved.

During the live broadcast, actively monitor the chat or comment section. Respond promptly to questions and comments, and address viewers by their names whenever possible. This personal touch shows that you truly value and appreciate their engagement. Additionally, try to incorporate their contributions into the show by highlighting interesting comments or addressing popular topics raised by the audience. This not only encourages continued participation but also makes your viewers feel like active contributors to the content.

Another powerful way to engage with your live audience is by featuring viewer-generated content. Encourage viewers to submit their own videos, ideas, or stories related to the show's theme. Incorporating user-generated content not only adds variety to your show but also creates a strong sense of inclusivity and community. By showcasing their contributions, you demonstrate that your audience is an integral part of the show's success.

Furthermore, consider hosting interactive segments during your webshow. From live polls to Q&A sessions, there are numerous ways to directly involve your audience. For example, you can ask viewers to vote on topics they want to see covered next, or invite them to submit questions or dilemmas to be addressed during a dedicated Q&A portion of the show.

By giving your audience opportunities to actively participate, you keep them invested and excited throughout the broadcast.

Lastly, after the live show concludes, make an effort to continue engaging with your viewers. Respond to any outstanding comments or questions you may have missed during the broadcast. Additionally, consider creating a dedicated space for ongoing discussions or feedback, such as a community forum or social media group. This enables your audience to connect with each other, creating a sense of camaraderie that extends beyond the webshow itself.

In conclusion, as a remarkable producer, I urge you to embrace the power of live engagement with your audience. By actively involving your viewers, responding to their contributions, and creating a sense of community, you'll foster long-lasting connections and cultivate a fiercely loyal following. Remember, it's not just about delivering compelling content, but about making each viewer feel like an essential part of the show's success.

Managing the technical aspects of live streaming can be intimidating at first, but fear not! With a little practice and some troubleshooting skills, you'll be a pro in no time. Familiarize yourself with the streaming software or platform you're using, learn how to set up scenes or overlays, and make sure to test your audio and video settings before going live. Technical hiccups are inevitable, so always have a backup plan and a sense of humor. Remember, even the most experienced streamers have had their fair share of "oops" moments!

As we wrap up this subchapter, keep in mind that live streaming and interactivity are ever-evolving mediums. Stay updated with the latest trends, experiment with new features, and continuously engage with your audience to keep them coming back for more. Your webshow is your canvas, so don't be afraid to unleash your creativity and have fun with it!

Now, let's take a moment to appreciate the fact that we live in a time where we can host webshows from the comfort of our homes, reaching audiences all around the world. It's like having your own TV station without the hefty production costs or the need for a fancy studio. So, grab your microphone, adjust your camera angle, and get ready to entertain, educate, and inspire your viewers through the power of live streaming and interactivity. It's showtime, folks!

4.4: Audience Engagement Strategies

In this exciting subchapter, we dive deep into the world of audience engagement strategies for your webshow. We all know that creating a webshow is one thing, but getting your audience to stick around and actively participate is a whole other ballgame. Luckily, we've got you covered with a treasure trove of strategies that will have your viewers hanging on to every word and eagerly awaiting your next episode.

One of the most effective ways to engage your audience is through Q&A sessions. These sessions not only allow your viewers to ask burning questions, but they also give you a chance to showcase your expertise and build a personal connection with your audience. So go ahead, embrace your inner talk show host and get ready to answer some thought-provoking questions!

Polls are another fantastic tool to keep your audience engaged. Not only do they provide valuable feedback, but they also make your viewers feel like they are an integral part of your webshow. Whether it's asking their opinion on a hot topic or getting their input on potential future guests, polls are a great way to make your audience feel heard and valued.

Now, let's talk giveaways. Who doesn't love free stuff? Hosting giveaways on your webshow is not only a fantastic way to reward your loyal viewers, but it also creates a buzz and excitement that can attract new audience members. From exclusive merchandise to tickets to exciting events, giveaways are a surefire way to keep your viewers coming back for more.

But it's not just about the tangible rewards. Creating a sense of community is crucial for audience engagement. By fostering a welcoming and inclusive environment, you encourage your viewers to become active participants in the webshow experience. Encourage them to interact with each other through comments and discussions, and watch as your audience transforms into a vibrant community that supports and uplifts each other.

Now, let's address the elephant in the room - audience feedback. It's easy to fall into the trap of thinking that you know exactly what your viewers want, but the truth is, their feedback is invaluable. Actively seek out their opinions and suggestions, and don't be afraid to adjust your content based on their input. Remember, your audience is the lifeblood of your webshow, and by listening to them, you're ensuring that your content remains relevant and exciting. I must emphasize the importance of audience feedback in creating exceptional content. It is the guiding force that propels a webshow to new heights of success and captures the hearts of viewers around the globe. So, dear creators, heed my words and embark on a journey of continuous improvement.

First and foremost, let us not overlook the fact that our viewers possess a diverse range of preferences, perspectives, and insights. They are the ones who invest their precious time into watching our webshow, and their opinions should be cherished. Forge a connection with them, for it is their engagement that fuels the fire of our creativity.

Embrace every review, comment, and suggestion with open arms. Foster a culture that welcomes constructive criticism, for it is within these moments of vulnerability that we learn, grow, and evolve. Actively seek out their opinions through surveys, social media polls, and interactive elements within the webshow itself. By doing so, you not only empower your audience but also create a sense of belonging and ownership.

However, do not merely accept feedback as a box to be checked. Instead, view it as a powerful tool for progress. Analyze the common threads and recurring themes in the feedback received. In doing so, you can unveil hidden patterns, identify areas for improvement, and tailor your content to better resonate with your audience's desires.

Moreover, never be afraid to experiment and push boundaries. Always keep an ear to the ground, listening for the whispers of change and innovation.

Adaptation is the key to remaining relevant and exciting in a swiftly evolving digital landscape. Inject fresh ideas and unexpected surprises into your webshow, while staying true to its core essence. It is this delicate balance that will captivate and surprise your audience, ensuring their continued loyalty.

Remember your audience is not just a passive witness to your content; they are active participants in your journey. Engage with them on a meaningful level, and they will reward you with their unwavering support, authenticity, and unwarranted admiration. Treat their feedback as the lighthouse that guides your ship, illuminating the path to greatness.

In conclusion, dear creators, embrace the elephant in the room - audience feedback. It is the compass that keeps your webshow on course, the wind that fills your sails, and the melody that resonates joyously across the virtual expanse. Let it guide your writing, ignite your storytelling, and inspire your creativity. By remaining attentive to the wants and needs of your viewers, you will create a masterpiece that will echo in the annals of digital history.

So there you have it, a comprehensive guide to audience engagement strategies for your webshow. From Q&A sessions to polls, giveaways, and creating a sense of community, these strategies will help you build a dedicated and enthusiastic audience. Remember, the key is to foster a connection with your viewers, make them feel valued, and keep them coming back for more.

Now, it's time to put these strategies into action and watch as your webshow reaches new heights of success. Happy engaging!

And hey, just a quick joke to lighten the mood - why don't scientists trust atoms? Because they make up everything!

4.5: Collaborating With Guests

In the vast world of webshows and podcasts, one thing is clear: collaborating with guests can take your content to new heights. Whether you're a seasoned host or just starting out, this subchapter is your guide to inviting and working with guests on your show. We'll dive into networking strategies, scheduling tips, and even preparing interview questions that will guarantee a successful episode. So grab your favorite beverage and let's get started!

Networking Strategies:

As a webshow host, it's essential to build a network of like-minded individuals who can bring value to your show. Start by attending industry events, joining online communities, and reaching out to potential guests through social media. Remember, networking is all about building genuine relationships, so approach it with a friendly and curious mindset. Don't be afraid to introduce yourself, engage in conversations, and express your interest in having them on your show. Who knows, your next guest might just be a tweet away! Once you have established a network of potential guests, it's time to start reaching out and inviting them onto your webshow. Craft a personalized message for each individual, demonstrating your genuine interest in their expertise and how you believe they can add value to your show. Be concise, respectful, and clear about the benefits they can expect from participating.

When you receive a positive response, take the time to schedule a pre-interview meeting or call. This not only allows you to build a rapport with your guest but also helps you prepare for the upcoming show. During this discussion, discuss the main topics to be covered, any specific questions you have in mind, and any requirements they may have.

In the days leading up to the show, promote your upcoming episode on your website, social media platforms, and email newsletters. Create excitement around the guest and the valuable insights they will share. Consider providing a sneak peek or teaser to increase interest and engagement.

As the day of the show approaches, ensure that all technical aspects are in place. Test your equipment, internet connection, and any necessary software. Additionally, prepare a professional-looking set or backdrop that reflects your show's branding and creates a visually appealing atmosphere.

When it's finally time for the interview, create a warm and relaxed environment for your guest. Start the show with an introduction that highlights their achievements and expertise. Engage in a friendly conversation, allowing them to share their unique insights while keeping the audience engaged. Utilize a mix of prepared questions and spontaneous follow-ups to ensure a dynamic and enjoyable interview.

Throughout the conversation, actively listen to your guest's responses and provide thoughtful commentary. Make sure to maintain a balance between showcasing their expertise and keeping the conversation flowing, ensuring that your audience can easily follow along and benefit from the discussion.

Once the interview is over, thank your guest for their participation and let them know when the episode will be published. Follow up with them to share the final product and express your gratitude for their valuable contribution.

Remember, networking isn't just a one-time endeavor. Foster these connections by continuing to engage with your guests and promoting their work even after the show. Share their content, comment on their posts, and look for opportunities to collaborate in the future. By nurturing these relationships, you'll not only expand your network but also cultivate long-lasting partnerships that can contribute to the growth and success of your webshow.

So, go forth with confidence, curiosity, and a genuine desire to connect with like-minded individuals. The world is waiting to hear the stories and expertise of your next guest, and your webshow is the perfect platform to bring them to life. Happy networking!

Scheduling Tips:

Once you've connected with potential guests, the next step is to find a mutually convenient time to record your episode. Scheduling can be a tricky task, especially when dealing with guests from different time zones or with busy schedules. To make things easier, consider using scheduling tools like Calendly or Doodle, which allow guests to choose from a selection of available time slots. Be flexible and accommodating, understanding that your guest's time is valuable. And don't forget to send a friendly reminder a few days before the recording to ensure everyone is on the same page.When it comes to scheduling, being organized and proactive is key. As the world's best writer, I know all too well the importance of punctuality and preparation. So, after finding potential guests and identifying the best ways to connect with them, it's time to tackle the scheduling challenge.

First and foremost, take into account the different

time zones of your guests. International collaborations are becoming more common, and coordinating schedules across continents can be quite the puzzle. To make this task easier, utilize the wonders of modern technology. Scheduling tools like Calendly or Doodle can be a lifesaver. Simply share a link with your guests that allows them to choose from a range of available time slots that work for both parties. This way, you eliminate the need for lengthy back-and-forth email exchanges and ensure a smoother scheduling process.

However, don't limit yourself solely to those tools. Creativity can go a long way! Consider other options like using a world clock app or a shared online calendar to help you visualize time zone differences and find a suitable time for recording. By being resourceful, you'll show your dedication to accommodating your guests and make working together a breeze.

Understanding that your guest's time is as valuable as your own is crucial. Be flexible and open-minded during the scheduling process. If a guest suggests a time that may be slightly inconvenient for you, try your best to find a compromise. Great collaborations are built on mutual respect and understanding, so showing your willingness to adapt will leave a lasting positive impression on your guests.

Once you've settled on a date and time, don't forget to send a friendly reminder a few days in advance. This ensures that everyone involved is on the same page and prevents any last-minute confusion. A simple email or even a quick message via your preferred communication platform will suffice. Remember, clear communication is key in any successful endeavor.

As a writer, I've learned that being organized, flexible, and respectful of others' time greatly contributes to building strong relationships. So, take these scheduling tips to heart and embark on your podcasting journey with confidence. With your exceptional content creation skills and dedication to professionalism, prepare for a recording session that exceeds all expectations.

Preparing Interview Questions:

Now comes the fun part - preparing your interview questions! A well-prepared set of questions can make or break an episode, so take the time to do your research on your guest and their expertise. Start with some icebreaker questions to set a relaxed and friendly tone. Then, move on to more specific and thought-provoking questions that will showcase your guest's knowledge and insights. Remember, it's essential to strike a balance between structure and spontaneity. Leave room for organic conversation and follow-up questions that arise during the interview. And hey, don't be afraid to throw in a lighthearted or unexpected question to keep things entertaining!

Begin by immersing yourself in the world of your guest. Delve into their accomplishments, their expertise, and their unique perspective. The more you understand their background, the better equipped you'll be to craft questions that unveil their true essence. Let their story unfold through your words, capturing the interest of your listeners from the very first question.

Icebreaker questions serve as the gateway to forging a comfortable and friendly atmosphere. They pave the way for genuine connection and allow your guest to relax and open up. From inquiring about their favorite childhood memory to asking them what they're currently binge-watching on Netflix, these questions set the tone for an engaging conversation.

But as you transition from icebreakers to the heart of the interview, it's time to don your thinking cap and bring out the big guns. Thought-provoking questions await, ones that will showcase the depths of your guest's knowledge and insights. Craft queries that challenge their perspectives, encouraging them to delve into the nuances of their field. Ask them to share their most profound experiences, the turning points that shaped them into the experts they are today.

Yet, dear writer, remember the delicate balance you must strike. Too much rigidity can stifle the organic flow of conversation, while too much spontaneity can lead to meandering tangents. Leave room for the unexpected, those unscripted moments that make an interview truly unforgettable. Allow yourself the flexibility to explore the uncharted territories that arise during the conversation. Embrace the art of the follow-up question, for it is there that the most insightful moments often reside.

And don't be afraid to inject a touch of levity into

the mix. A lighthearted or unexpected question can inject a delightful surprise into the interview, captivating both your guest and your audience. Perhaps you'll ask them about their guilty pleasure music or their favorite food combination that makes others cringe. These playful interludes can breathe life into an interview, reminding everyone involved that this is not just an exchange of knowledge, but a celebration of human connection.

A Successful Episode:

To ensure a successful episode, it's crucial to create a comfortable and welcoming environment for your guest. Start by doing a brief introduction before diving into the questions. Make your guest feel valued and appreciated by acknowledging their expertise and achievements. During the interview, actively listen to their responses, asking follow-up questions to delve deeper into the topic. Remember, collaboration is a two-way street, so encourage your guest to ask questions or share their own insights. Finally, wrap up the episode by expressing gratitude and giving your guest an opportunity to promote any upcoming projects or social media handles.

With these insights on inviting and collaborating with guests, you're well on your way to creating engaging and memorable episodes for your webshow. Remember to network, schedule wisely, prepare thoughtful questions, and create a comfortable environment for your guests. By following these tips, you'll not only have fantastic content but also build valuable connections within your industry. So, go forth, invite those guests, and let the collaboration begin! Happy podcasting!

Chapter 6

Low-Cost
Maintenance

5.1: Equipment Maintenance and Upgrades

In this subchapter, we dive deep into the world of equipment maintenance and upgrades for podcasting and video production. We all know that technology can be a fickle friend, but fear not! With the right tips and tricks, you'll be able to extend the lifespan of your equipment and avoid any unexpected hiccups along the way.

Let's start by talking about routine maintenance. Just like how you take care of yourself with a balanced diet and exercise (or at least attempt to), your podcasting and video production equipment needs some TLC too. First and foremost, make sure to keep your gear clean. Dust and debris can wreak havoc on your equipment, so be sure to wipe down your microphones, cameras, and other devices regularly. And don't forget to clean your cables too! They may not be the star of the show, but they play a vital role in keeping everything connected.

Now, let's move on to troubleshooting common issues. We've all been there, frantically trying to fix a technical glitch moments before a live stream or recording session. It's a special kind of panic, isn't it? But fear not, my friend! Here are a few common issues and their quick fixes:

1. **Audio issues:** If you're experiencing crackling or muffled sound, check your microphone connections first. Ensure that everything is securely plugged in and that there are no loose cables. If the problem persists, try using a different microphone or adjusting your audio settings.

2. **Video quality problems:** Is your video looking pixelated or blurry? Don't worry, it's not your eyes playing tricks on you. Start by checking your camera settings and make sure you're capturing at the highest resolution possible. If that doesn't do the trick, consider upgrading your camera or investing in better lighting equipment.

3. **Internet woes:** Slow internet speeds can be the bane of a podcaster or streamer's existence. If you're experiencing lag or buffering during live streams, try connecting your device directly to your router with an Ethernet cable. If that's not an option, consider

upgrading your internet plan or investing in a Wi-Fi range extender to improve your signal strength.

Now, let's talk about everyone's favorite topic: budget-friendly upgrade options. We all love shiny new gadgets, but our wallets often have a different opinion. Luckily, there are plenty of ways to upgrade your equipment without breaking the bank. Here are a few ideas:

1. **Second-hand gear:** Check out online marketplaces or local classifieds for second-hand equipment. Many podcasters and video producers upgrade their gear regularly, so you might just find a gem at a fraction of the cost.

2. **DIY solutions:** Get your creative juices flowing and try building your own equipment. From homemade soundproofing panels to DIY camera stabilizers, the internet is filled with tutorials and guides for budget-friendly projects that can enhance your production quality.

3. **Software upgrades:** Don't underestimate the power of software. Before splurging on new hardware, explore the world of plugins and editing software. They can often breathe new life into your recordings and videos, giving them that professional touch without breaking the bank.

Remember, my fellow podcasters and streamers, taking care of your equipment is the key to long-lasting success. So grab that microfiber cloth and get ready to conquer the world of maintenance and upgrades. And if all else fails, just remember that duct tape fixes everything – except maybe a broken heart. But that's a topic for another book. Stay tuned, my friends!

5.2: Free and Affordable Software Alternatives

In today's digital age, technology has become an integral part of our lives, especially when it comes to creating content. Whether you're a podcaster, a streamer, or a student looking to start your own web-show, having the right software tools is essential. But let's face it, not everyone has the budget to invest in expensive software. That's where free and affordable alternatives come in to save the day!

In this subchapter, we'll explore a range of free and low-cost alternatives for podcast editing soft-ware, graphic design tools, video editing software, and project management tools. These alternatives offer a wide range of features and benefits, allowing you to create professional-quality content without breaking the bank.

Let's start with podcast editing software. While industry-standard software like Adobe Audition and Pro Tools may be out of reach for many, there are fantastic free options available. One such alternative is Audacity, a powerful open-source software that offers a plethora of editing tools. With Audacity, you can easily edit your podcast episodes, remove background noise, and even apply special effects. Plus, it's beginner-friendly, so you don't need to be a tech wizard to use it!

Now, let's dive into graphic design tools. Creating eye-catching logos and intros is crucial for branding your podcast or webshow. While software like Adobe Photoshop and Illustrator can be expensive, there are cost-effective alternatives like Canva and GIMP. Canva is a user-friendly online design platform that offers a wide range of templates, fonts, and graphics. GIMP, on the other hand, is a powerful open-source image editing software that can rival even the most expensive options. With these tools, you can create stunning visuals to captivate your audience.

Next up, video editing software. If you're planning to create video content for your webshow or podcast, having a reliable video editing tool is a must. While software like Adobe Premiere Pro and Final Cut Pro are widely used in the industry, they come with a hefty price tag. Thankfully, there are affordable alternatives like Shotcut and DaVinci Resolve. Shotcut is an intuitive open-source video editor that offers a wide range of features, including transitions, filters, and color grading. DaVinci Resolve, on the other hand, is a professional-grade software that is available in both free and paid versions. With these tools, you can edit and enhance your videos like a pro.

Last but not least, project management tools. Whether you're working on your podcast or webshow solo or with a team, staying organized is key. While software like Trello and Asana offer excellent project management features, they may not fit everyone's budget. Luckily, there are affordable alternatives like Notion and ClickUp. Notion is an all-in-one workspace that allows you to organize your tasks, notes, and files in a visually pleasing and collaborative manner. ClickUp, on the other hand, is a comprehensive project management tool that offers a wide range of features, including task tracking, team collaboration, and time management. With these tools, you can stay on top of your projects and ensure everything runs smoothly.

So, there you have it – a range of free and affordable software alternatives for podcast editing, graphic design, video editing, and project management. With these tools at your disposal, you can create amazing content without breaking the bank. Remember, it's not always about the price tag – it's about the creativity and passion you put into your work. So go ahead, unleash your creativity, and let these software alternatives be your secret weapons in the world of content creation!

And hey, if anyone asks you how you managed to create such professional content on a budget, just tell them it's a little something called "tech-savvy wizardry" – and maybe throw in a wink for good measure!

5.3: Leveraging Free Online Resources

In today's digital age, where every penny counts, it's crucial to find ways to minimize expenses when starting and running a podcast or webshow. Luckily, the internet is teeming with free resources that can help you in your creative endeavors without breaking the bank. This subchapter, 5.3: Leveraging Free Online Resources, explores various platforms and websites that offer free music, sound effects, stock images, royalty-free footage, and even website hosting. So, grab your metaphorical backpack and let's embark on a journey to uncover these hidden treasures!

First up on our freebie extravaganza is the world of free music. Now, we all know that music is the key to setting the right mood and capturing your audience's attention. But fret not, my fellow creators, for there are platforms like FreeMusicArchive and Incompetech that offer a wide range of royalty-free tunes. Whether you're looking for an epic orchestral piece or a funky jazz number, these websites have got you covered. So, instead of shelling out your hard-earned cash for expensive licenses, you can now bask in the glory of free, high-quality music.

But wait, there's more! Sound effects can add that extra oomph to your podcast or webshow. Whether it's the sound of thunder for a dramatic moment or the chirping of birds to transport your listeners to a serene forest, sound effects can truly elevate your content. Websites like Freesound and ZapSplat offer an extensive collection of free sound effects that can take your production value to new heights. So, go ahead and sprinkle some audio magic into your episodes without spending a dime.

Now, let's talk visuals. A picture is worth a thousand words, and in the world of podcasting and webshows, visuals are essential to grabbing your audience's attention. Luckily, there are platforms like Unsplash and Pixabay that provide an array of stunning stock images that are completely free to use. So, instead of spending hours on end searching for the perfect visual representation or emptying your wallet on expensive stock photography, you can now browse through these treasure troves of images and find the perfect match for your content.

But what about videos? Fear not, my friend, for royalty-free footage is also at your fingertips. Platforms like Pexels and Videvo offer a vast selection of free stock footage that can add that professional touch to your webshow without the hefty price tag. Whether you need a sweeping aerial shot or a close-up of a cooking process, these websites have a variety of clips that can help you tell your story visually. So, unleash your inner Spielberg and dive into the world of free video resources.

Last but certainly not least, let's talk about website hosting. In today's digital landscape, having a website is crucial for establishing your online presence. However, hosting fees can add up quickly, especially for those on a tight budget. Luckily, platforms like Word-Press.com and Wix offer free website hosting options that allow you to create and customize your own website without spending a dime. With user-friendly interfaces and a wide range of templates, you can design a sleek and professional website that show-cases your podcast or webshow to the world.

Now, I know what you're thinking, "How do these platforms make money if everything is free?" Well, my friend, many of these websites offer premium options or rely on advertising revenue to sustain their operations. So, while you can enjoy the benefits of these free resources, you also have the option to upgrade to premium features or support these platforms through other means if you so choose.

In conclusion, the internet is a treasure trove of free resources just waiting to be discovered. By leveraging these platforms for free music, sound effects, stock images, royalty-free footage, and website hosting, you can minimize expenses while still creating high-quality content for your podcast or webshow. So, go forth and explore the vast landscape of the internet, my fellow creators. Your wallet will thank you, and your audience will be captivated by the brilliance of your creations. And remember, the best things in life are often free – just like these online resources!

5.4: Outsourcing and Automation

Outsourcing and automation, my friends, are like the dynamic duo of the podcasting and webshow world. They swoop in to save the day, taking care of those tedious tasks that eat up your time and energy. Editing, graphic design, social media management –

these are the tasks that can make or break your show, and finding reliable and cost-effective options can feel like searching for a unicorn in a haystack. But fear not, for I am here to guide you through this subchapter and help you navigate the world of outsourcing and automation.

Let's start with outsourcing, shall we? Picture this: you're knee-deep in audio files, desperately trying to edit out all those "ums" and "uhs" that seem to have multiplied overnight. Your eyes are tired, your fingers are sore, and you're pretty sure you've lost your sanity somewhere along the way. Enter the freelancer, your knight in shining armor. By outsourcing your editing tasks to a skilled professional, you can free up your time and energy to focus on the aspects of podcasting that truly light your fire.

Now, finding a reliable freelancer can be a bit like finding a needle in a haystack. But fear not, my friends, for I have a few tricks up my sleeve. First, do your research. Take the time to read reviews, ask for recommendations, and stalk their social media profiles (in a non-creepy way, of course). Second, don't be afraid to test the waters. Start with a small project to see if the freelancer's style and work ethic align with your vision. And finally, communicate, communicate, communicate. Clear and open lines of communication are key to a successful outsourcing relationship. So don't be shy – speak up and let your freelancer know what you need and expect.

But what about those tasks that don't require a

human touch? Enter automation, the unsung hero of the digital age. Automation tools can be a game-changer when it comes to graphic design, social media management, and even guest outreach. Imagine having a virtual assistant that schedules your social media posts, creates eye-catching graphics, and even reaches out to potential guests on your behalf. It's like having your own personal army of robots working tirelessly behind the scenes while you sip a margarita on a tropical beach. Okay, maybe not exactly like that, but you get the idea.

Now, I know what you're thinking – won't automation make my show lose that personal touch? And that's a valid concern, my friends. While automation can certainly streamline your processes and save you time, it's important to strike a balance. You don't want your show to sound like it's been produced by a cold, heartless machine. So my advice? Use automation as a tool, not a crutch. Let it handle the repetitive tasks, but don't forget to add your personal touch to the things that matter most – your content, your inter-actions with guests, and your connection with your audience.

So, my fellow podcasters and webshow enthusiasts, outsourcing and automation are the secret weapons that can take your show to the next level. They're like the Robin to your Batman, the peanut butter to your jelly – you get the picture. So go forth, my friends, and embrace the power of outsourcing and automation. Your show will thank you, your audience will thank you, and I'll thank you for keeping me entertained with your amazing content. And hey, if you ever need someone to test out your margarita recipes, you know where to find me. Cheers!

5.5: Budgeting and Financial Planning

Budgeting and financial planning may not sound like the most exciting topics, but trust me, they are essential for any podcaster or webshow creator. After all, if you want to keep your show running smoothly and even make some money from it, you need to know where your money is coming from and where it's going. So, grab your calculator and let's dive into the world of budgeting and financial planning!

First things first, let's talk about budgeting for podcasting or webshow expenses. You might be thinking, "But wait, I thought starting a podcast or webshow was supposed to be low-cost?" Well, my friend, while it's true that you can start with a minimal budget, there are still expenses to consider. Equipment, hosting fees, editing software, and even promotional materials all come with a price tag. But fear not, with some careful planning and budgeting, you can keep those costs under control.

Start by listing all your expenses. Break them down into categories like equipment, software, hosting, and marketing. Research the costs associated with each item and add them up. This will give you a clear picture of how much money you'll need to get started and keep your show running smoothly. Don't forget to include any recurring expenses, like monthly hosting fees or software subscriptions.

Now, let's move on to tracking your income and expenses. It's important to know where your money is coming from and how much you're spending. This will help you make informed decisions about your show's finances and identify areas where you can cut costs or find new revenue streams.

Create a simple spreadsheet or use a budgeting app to track your income and expenses. Make sure to update it regularly, so you always have an accurate picture of your financial situation. Be diligent about recording every expense, no matter how small. Those little costs can add up quickly!

Now, let's talk about monetization opportunities. This is where the magic happens – turning your podcast or webshow into a money-making machine! There are various ways to monetize your show, and it's essential to explore different options to cover your expenses and generate income.

One popular monetization method is advertising. You can partner with brands and companies that align with your show's niche and values. You can also explore affiliate marketing, where you earn a commission for promoting products or services on your show. Another option is to offer premium content or create a membership program for your loyal fans. The possibilities are endless, so get creative and find the right monetization strategy for your show.

Remember, budgeting and financial planning are ongoing processes. As your show grows and evolves, your expenses and income will change. It's crucial to review and adjust your budget regularly to stay on track. And hey, don't be afraid to dream big! Who knows, maybe one day your podcast or webshow will be a financial success.

So, my fellow podcaster or webshow creator, don't let the numbers scare you. Embrace the world of budgeting and financial planning, and you'll set yourself up for success. And remember, if all else fails, just throw in a few jokes to lighten the mood. After all, laughter is the best budgeting hack!

Chapter 7

Low-Cost Promotion

ers. Think of it as the cover of your podcast or webshow, the first thing people see before they decide whether to click or scroll past. So, how do you create an engaging thumbnail? Well, fear not, for I shall bestow upon you the secrets of the trade.

First and foremost, keep it visually appealing. Choose images or graphics that accurately represent the essence of your episode. If you're discussing the latest advancements in quantum physics, don't slap a picture of a cute kitten on your thumbnail (unless, of course, you can find a way to make Schrödinger's cat relevant). Aim for clarity and coherence, making sure your thumbnail aligns with the topic and vibe of your content.

Your thumbnail should be a captivating visual

synopsis, enticing viewers to click and explore your episode further. Consider using bold colors, dynamic compositions, or intriguing elements that pique curiosity. Remember, the thumbnail is the first impression of your content, so make it count.

Next, craft an engaging title that grabs attention and accurately reflects the episode's essence. Avoid generic titles like "Quantum Physics Advancements" and instead opt for something like "Unraveling the Mysteries of Quantum Reality" or "Quantum Leaps: Breaking Down the Latest Discoveries." Play with words, add a touch of intrigue, and create a sense of anticipation for what's to come.

Once viewers are enticed by your thumbnail and title, it's crucial to deliver on their expectations. Structure your episode in a coherent and logical manner, allowing the content to flow smoothly from one idea to the next. Consider using visual aids such as diagrams, animations, or footage that support your narrative and enhance comprehension.

To further engage your audience, infuse your episode with anecdotal stories, real-life examples, or thought-provoking questions. These elements humanize complex topics and make them relatable. Additionally, strive to find a balance between expert knowledge and accessibility, ensuring that viewers of all backgrounds and expertise can grasp the core ideas.

Throughout your episode, maintain a conversational tone that keeps viewers invested. Avoid relying too heavily on technical jargon or complicated terminology unless it is necessary for clarity and accuracy. Break down complex concepts into digestible pieces, using analogies or metaphors to illustrate abstract ideas in a more relatable manner.

Finally, conclude your episode with a strong, memorable ending. Recap the key points discussed, leaving viewers with a sense of satisfaction and a desire to explore the topic further. Consider adding a call-to-action, encouraging viewers to share their thoughts, ask questions, or continue the conversation on your social media platforms.

Remember, as the world's best writer, your ultimate goal is to educate, entertain, and captivate your audience. By keeping your content visually appealing, coherent, and engaging, you will undoubtedly leave a lasting impact, sparking curiosity and fostering a love for learning in your viewers. So go forth and create remarkable episodes that will inspire, enlighten, and change the way people see the world.

Now, let's talk about promotional banners. These are like the billboards of the digital world, grabbing attention and conveying your message in a single glance. Whether you're promoting your upcoming episode or highlighting a special guest, a well-designed banner can work wonders. But here's the secret sauce: keep it simple yet eye-catching. Don't overcrowd it with too much information or cluttered visuals. Instead, focus on a bold headline, striking imagery, and perhaps a sprinkle of humor to grab attention.

Teaser videos are another powerful tool in your visual content arsenal. These short, snappy clips give potential listeners a taste of what's to come, leaving them craving more. Much like a movie trailer, a teaser video should pique curiosity, build anticipation, and leave viewers yearning for the full experience. Get creative with editing techniques, add some catchy music, and tease just enough to leave them wanting more. But remember, my dear content creator, don't give away all the juicy bits - leave some surprises for the actual episode.

Now, I can already hear some of you frantically Googling expensive design software and worrying about draining your bank account. Fear not, for I am here to save the day with a treasure trove of free or low-cost tools. The internet is a veritable smorgasbord of design resources, my friends. Canva, Adobe Spark, and GIMP are just a few examples of platforms that offer user-friendly interfaces and a plethora of templates and design elements at your disposal. So go forth, my fellow creators, and conquer the visual realm without breaking the bank!

With these affordable design tools at your fingertips, you possess the power to unleash your creativity and transform your ideas into visually stunning masterpieces. Canva, the beloved darling of the design world, allows even the most novice artist to effortlessly craft eye-catching graphics. Its intuitive interface and extensive template library make it a go-to choice for all your design needs.

If Canva is a gentle whisper, then Adobe Spark roars like a mighty lion. This powerful platform takes your designs to the next level with its array of stunning visuals and professional-grade features. From sleek social media graphics to captivating videos, Adobe Spark thrives on elevating your creations with a touch of awe-inspiring magic.

But let us not forget the unsung hero, GIMP. This open-source gem offers a wealth of tools akin to its more expensive counterparts, granting you full control over your artistic visions. With GIMP in your arsenal, you can break down barriers and bring your wildest dreams to life, all without draining your bank account.

Armed with these design tools, the world is your canvas, waiting to be painted with imaginative brilliance. So take a deep breath, my fellow creators, as you embark on this visual adventure. Embrace the countless possibilities that lie before you, and watch as your ideas take flight, capturing hearts and minds with their sheer beauty.

Do not let your financial worries hinder your journey into the realm of design. The internet has bestowed upon us a treasure trove of resources, providing even the humblest of budgets with the means to create captivating visuals. Free your mind from worry, and let your imagination soar as you make use of these affordable design tools.

Now, my friends, it is time for you to harness this power and conquer the visual realm. Unleash your creativity, pour your heart into your designs, and leave an indelible mark on the world. With these free or low-cost tools, there are no limits to what you can achieve.

So go forth, my fellow creators, armed with Canva, Adobe Spark, GIMP, and the burning desire to bring your artistic visions to life. Embrace the limitless potential of the internet's smorgasbord of design resources. And most importantly, remember to have fun along the way, for it is in that joyous state of creation that true mastery is born.

Creating compelling visual content is not just about making things pretty; it's about connecting with your audience on a deeper level. It's about conveying the essence of your podcast or webshow in a single image, banner, or video. So, don't underestimate the power of visuals in your promotional endeavors.

Remember, when it comes to creating visually appealing content, clarity and coherence are key. Embrace the magic of episode thumbnails, promotional banners, and teaser videos. And fear not, my dear creators, for the tools you need are at your fingertips, waiting to unleash your creative potential.

Now, armed with the knowledge of visual content wizardry, go forth and conquer the digital landscape. May your thumbnails be enticing, your banners be captivating, and your teaser videos be downright tantalizing. Happy creating, my friends, and may your podcasts and webshows flourish like never before!

6.5: Analyzing Promotion Strategies

In the world of podcasting and webshows, promotion is the lifeblood of success. You can have the most entertaining and informative content out there, but if no one knows about it, then what's the point? That's where analyzing promotion strategies comes into play. In this subchapter, we will dive deep into the importance of tracking and analyzing your promotional efforts, and how utilizing metrics and analytics tools can help measure the effectiveness of different strategies. So grab your data hat and let's get started!

First things first, why is analyzing promotion strategies so important? Well, imagine you're throwing a party. You spend hours planning the decorations, preparing the food, and curating the perfect playlist. But when the time comes, only a handful of people show up. What went wrong? Without analyzing your promotional efforts, it's like throwing a party blindfolded and hoping for the best. By tracking and analyzing your promotion strategies, you can gain valuable insights into what works and what doesn't, allowing you to make data-driven decisions and optimize future campaigns.

But how do you track and analyze your promotion efforts? Enter metrics and analytics tools. These powerful tools can provide you with a wealth of information about your audience, their behavior, and the effectiveness of your promotional strategies. From website traffic to social media engagement, metrics can give you a comprehensive view of how your promotions are performing.

For example, let's say you run a targeted Facebook ad campaign to promote your podcast. With metrics, you can track how many people clicked on your ad, how many converted into subscribers, and even analyze demographic data to see if your target audience aligns with your promotional efforts. Armed with this information, you can make informed decisions about where to allocate your promotional resources and optimize future campaigns.

Now, I know what you're thinking. "But tracking metrics and analyzing data sounds complicated and time-consuming!" Fear not, my fellow podcaster. There are a plethora of user-friendly analytics tools out there that can make this process a breeze. From Google Analytics to social media insights, these tools provide intuitive interfaces and actionable insights that even the tech-challenged among us can navigate.

So, let's take a moment to appreciate the power of data-driven decision-making. Remember, this isn't just about crunching numbers and looking at fancy charts (although that can be fun too). Analyzing promotion strategies allows you to understand your audience better, tailor your content to their preferences, and ultimately, drive more engagement and growth for your podcast or webshow.

Now, let's add a sprinkle of humor to lighten the mood. Imagine if tracking promotion efforts were like tracking your steps on a fitness app. Every time you promote your podcast or webshow, you earn "promotion points." And just like hitting your step goal for the day, reaching your promotion points goal would give you a sense of accomplishment and validation. Who said promoting your content can't be as satisfying as hitting 10,000 steps?

In all seriousness, though, analyzing promotion strategies is crucial for any podcaster or webshow host. It allows you to measure the impact of your efforts, identify areas for improvement, and ultimately, optimize your promotion campaigns for maximum reach and engagement. So, don't shy away from the data. Embrace it, learn from it, and let it guide you on your journey to podcasting and webshow success.

In the next subchapter, we will explore the exciting world of logo and intro design. From creating a visually captivating logo to crafting an engaging and memorable intro, we'll delve into the art of branding your podcast or webshow. Get ready to make a lasting impression!

Chapter 8

Engaging an Audience

7.1: Effective Communication Strategies

In this subchapter, we delve into the world of communication channels and explore how podcasters and webshow hosts can establish a direct line of communication with their audience. Effective communication is key to building a loyal and engaged following, and we'll discuss various strategies to help you achieve just that.

One of the most common communication channels for podcasters and webshow hosts is email newsletters. Now, I know what you're thinking – newsletters may seem a bit old-fashioned in the age of social media and instant messaging. But trust me, they still pack a punch! By sending out regular newsletters, you can provide updates on new episodes, share behind-the-scenes stories, and even offer exclusive content to your subscribers.

Think of your newsletter as a secret club, where your most dedicated fans can get an inside scoop on your show. And the best part? You don't have to be a tech wizard to set up an email newsletter. There are plenty of user-friendly platforms out there that make it a breeze to create and send newsletters – even for us non-tech-savvy folks.With just a few simple steps, you can embark on the journey of creating an irresistible email newsletter that will captivate your audience. So, let's dive right in and unlock the secrets to crafting a remarkable newsletter that will have your fans eagerly awaiting each new edition.

First, select a platform that caters to your specific needs. There's an array of user-friendly platforms available, such as Mailchimp, ConvertKit, or Constant Contact, which offer intuitive interfaces and pre-designed templates to make your newsletter creation process a breeze. These platforms also allow you to personalize your newsletters with your own branding, ensuring that it aligns seamlessly with your show's identity.

Once you've chosen your desired platform, it's time to curate captivating content. Think about what makes your show unique and why your fans are so dedicated. Is it exclusive behind-the-scenes footage, interviews with cast members or creators, or perhaps sneak peeks into upcoming episodes? Tailor your content to provide a genuine insider experience, giving your subscribers a sense of belonging to an exclusive club.

To keep your newsletter engaging, consider incorporating interactive elements. Including polls, questionnaires, or interactive quizzes will not only entertain your readers but also gather valuable insights about their preferences. Invite them to interact, share their opinions, and feel like active participants in your show's journey.

Furthermore, don't underestimate the power of visuals. Choose eye-catching images, captivating graphics, or even short video snippets to enhance the overall appeal of your newsletter. Remember, a picture is worth a thousand words, and in this case, it might just entice your fans to tune in to your show even more eagerly.

As you progress with your newsletter journey, don't forget about regularity. Consistency is key, as it builds anticipation and loyalty among your subscribers. Set a realistic schedule, whether it's weekly, bi-weekly, or monthly, and stick to it. Your fans will appreciate the reliability and eagerly anticipate each new edition, feeling like they are valuable members of your secret club.

Lastly, but crucially, engage with your audience. Encourage them to share their thoughts, feedback, and suggestions. Respond to their comments and create a sense of community. This personal connection will foster a deep sense of loyalty, making your fans feel like cherished insiders, a part of something special.

So, unlock the power of an email newsletter and step into the world of creating an exclusive club for your most dedicated fans. Harness the user-friendly platforms, curate captivating content, add interactivity, and engage with your subscribers. With each edition of your remarkable newsletter, you will deepen the bond between your show and its fans, creating an unforgettable experience that will leave them yearning for more.

Next up, let's talk about social media engagement. Ah, social media – the land of endless possibilities and cat videos. When used effectively, platforms like Twitter, Instagram, and Facebook can be powerful tools for connecting with your audience. But here's the secret sauce – it's not just about posting random updates and hoping for the best. You need to have a solid social media strategy in place.

Consistency is key when it comes to social media. Make sure to post regularly and engage with your audience by responding to comments and messages. But here's a pro tip – don't just use social media as a broadcasting platform. Take the time to listen to your audience, ask for their feedback, and genuinely connect with them. After all, a podcast or webshow is a two-way street, and building relationships with your listeners/viewers is crucial.

Now, let's talk about direct messaging. Whether it's through email or social media, direct messaging is a fantastic way to establish a personal connection with your audience. It's like having a one-on-one conversation with your listeners/viewers. And here's where authenticity comes into play.

In a world full of filters and perfectly curated content, it's refreshing to be real. Be yourself – quirks and all. Show your audience that you're not just a voice or a face on a screen, but a real person with thoughts, feelings, and the occasional messy hair day. Trust me, people appreciate authenticity, and it will help you build a loyal and engaged following.

Now, I know what you're thinking – "But how do I juggle all these communication channels while maintaining consistency?" Great question, dear reader! The answer lies in being organized and having a clear communication plan.

Set aside specific times each week to work on your email newsletters, schedule social media posts in advance, and allocate time for direct messaging. By establishing a routine and sticking to it, you'll ensure that your communication efforts are consistent and effective. Consistency is key when it comes to maintaining effective communication with your audience. By setting aside specific times each week to work on your email newsletters, you can ensure they are well-crafted and tailored to your readers' needs. Plan ahead by brainstorming ideas, researching relevant topics, and outlining the content you want to include. This way, when your scheduled newsletter creation time arrives, you can dive right in without wasting valuable creative energy.

In addition to email newsletters, social media is another powerful tool for reaching and engaging your audience. Consistency is equally important here. Schedule posts in advance so that you can maintain a consistent presence on your chosen platforms, while still allowing yourself time for real-time interactions. Use social media management tools to plan your content calendar, create eye-catching graphics, and draft captivating captions. By taking care of these tasks in advance, you can focus on building meaningful connections rather than scrambling to come up with last-minute posts.

Direct messaging is another crucial aspect of communication that shouldn't be neglected. Whether it's responding to customer inquiries, collaborating with industry peers, or simply engaging with your audience, allocating specific time for direct messaging is essential. Set aside regular blocks of time throughout the week to check your messages, respond promptly, and provide thoughtful, personalized responses. By doing so, you can demonstrate your dedication to customer service and foster deeper connections with your audience.

Remember, consistency and routine are the guiding principles for effective communication. By adhering to a schedule, you can ensure that each aspect of your communication efforts receives the attention it deserves. Whether it's crafting compelling email newsletters, scheduling engaging social media posts, or responding to direct messages, each task plays a vital role in building a strong and loyal audience. Embrace this routine and watch as your communication efforts soar to new heights, gaining the attention and admiration of your readers and followers.

In conclusion, effective communication is the backbone of any successful podcast or webshow. By utilizing different communication channels like email newsletters, social media engagement, and direct messaging, you can establish a direct line of communication with your audience. Remember, consistency and authenticity are key. So, go forth, dear podcasters and webshow hosts, and connect with your audience in the most engaging and genuine way possible.

7.2: Building a Community

Building a dedicated community of listeners or viewers around your podcast or webshow is crucial for long-term success and growth. Not only does it provide a loyal fanbase, but it also creates a sense of belonging and connection that keeps people coming back for more. In this subchapter, we will delve into the strategies and tactics that can help you build and nurture a thriving community around your content.

One of the first steps in building a community is creating a forum where your listeners or viewers can interact with each other and with you. This can be as simple as setting up a Facebook group or a dedicated forum on your website. Encourage discussions, ask for feedback, and foster a sense of community spirit. Remember, a community is not just about you, it's about the people who support and engage with your content. By providing a space for them to connect and share their thoughts, you are fostering a sense of belonging and encouraging them to become invested in your success.

In addition to creating a forum, hosting live events can be a game-changer for building a community. Whether it's a live podcast recording, a Q&A session, or a virtual hangout, these events provide an opportunity for your audience to interact with you in real-time. Not only does this foster a deeper connection, but it also gives you a chance to showcase your personality and build trust with your community. Plus, it's a great way to have some fun and inject a dose of excitement into your content!

Engagement is key when it comes to building a community, and one effective way to nurture engagement is through contests or challenges. Encourage your listeners or viewers to participate in competitions related to your content, such as caption contests or fan art challenges. Not only does this create a sense of friendly competition, but it also incentivizes your community to actively engage with your content and spread the word to others. Plus, who doesn't love the chance to win some cool prizes?

Now, let's take a moment to address the elephant in the room – trolls. Unfortunately, in any online community, there will always be a few individuals who thrive on negativity and seek to disrupt the harmony. As a content creator and community builder, it's important to have a plan in place to deal with these trolls. Encourage a positive and supportive atmosphere within your community, and be proactive in addressing any negative comments or behavior. Remember, your community is a reflection of your brand, so don't be afraid to take a firm stance and show that you won't tolerate toxic behavior.

In this digital age where the power of words can pierce through screens and leave scars on hearts, becoming a master of handling trolls is not an option but a necessity. As the world's best writer, allow me to shed light on a few strategies to conquer these digital shadows.

Firstly, fostering a positive and supportive atmosphere within your community is vital. Lead by example and ensure that mutual respect and kindness are the cornerstones of your online space. Encourage constructive discussions, feedback, and celebrate the accomplishments of your community members. By promoting positivity, you create a shield against the corrosive influence of trolls.

However, even with the most nurturing environment, trolls may still slink their way into your online sanctuary, sniffing for opportunities to sow discord. In such circumstances, it is essential to be proactive in addressing their negative comments or behavior. Swift action is required, not only to protect your community but also to convey a clear message that you take the wellbeing of your members seriously.

Implement clear guidelines and community standards that explicitly state what is acceptable behavior and what will not be tolerated. Educate your community on these standards, ensuring that everyone understands the expectations. By preemptively setting boundaries, you establish a firm ground that trolls can't easily invade.

When faced with a troll, respond with grace, but firmly. Engage them tactfully, focusing on defusing the situation rather than engaging in a back-and-forth battle. In doing so, you prevent their toxic comments from gaining traction. Remember, trolls feed on reactions, and denying them that satisfaction weakens their power.

Additionally, establish a reporting system so community members can easily flag any inappropriate behavior. Respond promptly to their reports and investigate thoroughly. By swiftly addressing the concerns of your community, you send a resounding message that their safety and wellbeing come first.

As the world's best writer, I remind you that your community is an extension of your brand. Thus, it is crucial to protect its integrity by taking a strong stance against toxic behavior. Implement consequences for repeated instances of trolling, such as temporary or permanent bans from your platforms. While it may seem harsh, it is necessary to maintain the integrity of your community and protect its genuine members.

Remember, trolls thrive in darkness, and the best way to combat them is by shining a light on their actions. Utilize your platform's algorithms and moderation tools to limit the visibility of their harmful comments. By giving prominence to positive interactions, you drown out the negativity and inspire others to follow suit.

In the vast landscape of the digital realm, trolls will always lurk in the shadows. But armed with these strategies, you can be the beacon of light that guides your community to a harmonious and supportive space. As a content creator and community builder, your words hold immeasurable power, and with that power comes the responsibility to shape a better online world for all.

In conclusion, building a dedicated community around your podcast or webshow is crucial for long-term success. By creating a forum, hosting live events, nurturing engagement through contests or challenges, and addressing trolls, you can foster a strong and supportive community that will not only keep coming back for more but will also help spread the word and attract new listeners or viewers. So go ahead, build your community brick by brick, and watch your podcast or webshow soar to new heights!

And remember, building a community is like planting a garden – it takes time, effort, and a little bit of humor. So, as you embark on this journey, don't forget to sprinkle in some jokes here and there. After all, laughter is the glue that binds a community together, and who doesn't want to be part of a community that knows how to have a good laugh? So go forth, my fellow content creators, and may your community bloom like a field of sunflowers on a sunny day!

7.3: Encouraging and Responding to Audience Feedback

In this exciting segment of our book, we dive headfirst into the world of audience feedback. Strap yourselves in, because we're about to embark on a journey that will not only enlighten you, but also equip you with the tools to engage and respond to your audience in the most constructive and engaging manner possible. Get ready for 7.3: Encouraging and Responding to Audience Feedback!

Now, you may be wondering, why is audience feedback so significant? Well, my fellow podcasters and webshow enthusiasts, audience feedback is the lifeblood of your content. It's like the fuel that keeps your creative engine running smoothly. Without feedback, your show can quickly become a one-way street, with you talking into the void and your audience left feeling unheard and unappreciated. We don't want that, do we? Of course not!

So, how do we encourage our listeners or viewers to provide feedback? It's all about creating an environment that fosters interaction and makes your audience feel valued. One fantastic method is to end each episode with a call to action. Ask your audience to share their thoughts, ideas, or questions in the comments section or through social media. Make it clear that their feedback is not only welcomed but eagerly anticipated. You could even sweeten the deal by offering incentives like shoutouts or exclusive content for those who actively engage with your show. Who doesn't love a good incentive, right?

Now, let's talk about responding to feedback. When someone takes the time to share their thoughts with you, it's essential to respond in a way that is both constructive and engaging. Remember, feedback is a gift, even if it sometimes feels like a lump of coal. So, instead of getting defensive or dismissing their opinions, embrace the opportunity for growth and improvement.

One strategy for responding to feedback is to start by expressing gratitude. Thank your audience member for taking the time to share their thoughts. It shows that you value their input and sets the stage for a positive exchange. Next, take a deep breath and remember that not all feedback is created equal. Some will be insightful and helpful, while others may be less so. Embrace the former and gently address the latter, offering suggestions or explanations that can help bridge the gap between their expectations and your creative vision.

Responding to feedback is not just about acknowledging and addressing criticism. It's also about celebrating the positive feedback and using it as fuel to keep doing what you love. When someone compliments your show, don't be shy about sharing their kind words with your audience. It not only boosts your own confidence but also lets your audience know that their feedback matters and can make a difference.The power of positive feedback should never be underestimated. It has the ability to uplift spirits, inspire greatness, and push artists to achieve even greater heights. As the curtains fall and the ovations pour in, it is vital to leverage those words of praise and share them with the world.

In the realm of theater, social media platforms serve as the perfect avenue to spread word of the kind reviews received. Craft a heartfelt post, a carefully woven tapestry of gratitude, to express your appreciation for the accolades you have received. Share the joy and excitement that you felt when reading such encouraging words, and extend that emotion to your loyal audience.

By shining a light on the positive feedback, you not only magnify the impact it made on you but also inspire others to support and engage with your work. Such transparency allows your audience to empathize with the journey you have undertaken, encouraging them to be an integral part of your artistic pursuit.

Remember, as artists, the feedback we receive—both positive and negative—should fuel our drive and passion. It should propel us forward, like a gentle breeze beneath our wings, pushing us to reach new horizons. Celebrating the positive feedback helps to reinforce this sentiment, reminding us that every step we take is not in vain; every word we speak, every note we hit, and every brushstroke we make has an impact.

Beyond simply fueling your individual ambitions, sharing kind words also strengthens the bond between artist and audience. It serves as a reminder that this journey is a shared one and that the audience plays a vital role in shaping and supporting the artwork. By acknowledging their impact, you demonstrate your appreciation for their trust, their presence, and their contributions to your artistic evolution.

However, amidst the celebration of positive feedback, it is important to remain humble and genuine. Gratitude should be the guiding force behind your actions, ensuring that the spotlight is not solely on you, but on the collective effort that goes into every masterpiece.

In conclusion, responding to feedback—both positive and negative—is an integral part of an artist's growth and evolution. When bestowed with kind words, use them as fuel and celebration of the passion that drives you. Share the praise with your audience, fostering a sense of unity and gratitude. Let their feedback be the guiding light on your artistic voyage, propelling you toward even greater heights.

So, my friends, as we wrap up this segment, remember that audience feedback is the secret sauce to creating a thriving podcast or webshow. Encourage your audience to share their thoughts and ideas, and respond to their feedback with grace and gratitude. Embrace the power of constructive criticism, and let the positive feedback propel you forward. With these strategies in your toolbox, you'll be well on your way to creating a show that not only captivates your audience but also builds a community that feels heard and valued. Happy feedback hunting!

7.4: Listener Interaction and Involvement

In the world of podcasting and webshows, one of the keys to success is engaging with your audience. After all, without listeners or viewers, what's the point, right? That's why in this subchapter, we're diving deep into the techniques that will help you actively involve your audience and keep them coming back for more.

So, let's kick things off with live Q&A sessions. Picture this: you're recording your podcast or webshow, and suddenly, a notification pops up from one of your loyal listeners. They have a burning question and want to know your thoughts. Instead of ignoring it or waiting until the end, why not address it right then and there? By conducting live Q&A sessions, you not only show your audience that you value their input, but you also create a sense of real-time interaction. Plus, it adds an element of excitement and unpredictability to your episodes. It's like having a virtual chat with your listeners, and trust me, they'll love it!

Now, let's talk about featuring listener-submitted stories or questions. Your audience is filled with diverse individuals who have unique experiences and perspectives. Why not tap into that goldmine and showcase their stories or answer their burning questions on your podcast or webshow? By doing so, you not only give your audience a chance to be heard, but you also create a sense of community. People love hearing stories from others who have gone through similar situations or have interesting tales to share. It adds a personal touch to your content and makes your audience feel like they're part of something bigger.

But what about incorporating audience suggestions into future episodes? Well, my friend, that's where the magic happens. Your audience is a treasure trove of ideas, and by actively seeking their suggestions, you not only show that you value their input, but you also ensure that your content remains relevant and engaging. It's like having a team of creative collaborators who are just as passionate about your podcast or webshow as you are. So, don't be afraid to ask your audience what they want to hear or see in future episodes. Who knows, they might just come up with a brilliant idea that takes your show to the next level!

Now, let's sprinkle in some humor, shall we? Imagine this scenario: you're recording your podcast, and suddenly, you receive a hilarious comment from one of your listeners. Instead of chuckling to yourself and moving on, why not share it with your audience? By injecting humor into your episodes, you not only entertain your listeners, but you also create a light-hearted and enjoyable atmosphere. After all, who doesn't love a good laugh? So, don't be afraid to let your comedic side shine through. Trust me, your audience will appreciate it and keep coming back for more.

So, there you have it, my fellow podcasters and webshow hosts. In this subchapter, we've explored techniques to actively involve your audience. From conducting live Q&A sessions to featuring listener-submitted stories or questions, and incorporating audience suggestions into future episodes, the possibilities are endless. Remember, your audience is the lifeblood of your show, so make sure to keep them engaged, entertained, and involved. Happy podcasting and webshow hosting!

7.5: Building Long-Term Relationships

In the fast-paced world of podcasting and web-shows, it's easy to get caught up in the excitement of creating and producing content. But one aspect that is often overlooked, yet crucial to long-term success, is building and nurturing relationships with your audience. In this subchapter, we will dive into the importance of cultivating these relationships and explore strategies for consistently delivering valuable content, showing appreciation, and exploring collaboration opportunities or exclusive perks.

First and foremost, consistently delivering valuable content is key to capturing and retaining the attention of your audience. Think of your content as a gift to your listeners or viewers – something that they eagerly anticipate and find value in. Whether it's thought-provoking discussions, entertaining interviews, or informative tutorials, make sure your content is relevant, engaging, and addresses the needs and interests of your target audience. Remember, your listeners or viewers are investing their time and attention in you, so it's important to consistently deliver content that is worth their while.

But delivering valuable content alone is not enough. Showing appreciation for your audience's support is equally important. Imagine if you had a friend who always took you for granted and never acknowledged your support – you'd start to question the value of that relationship, right? The same principle applies to your relationship with your audience. Take the time to thank your listeners or viewers for their support, whether it's through social media shout-outs, personalized emails, or even sending them small tokens of appreciation. By showing gratitude, you not only strengthen your connection with your audience but also make them feel valued and appreciated.

Another way to build long-term relationships with your audience is by exploring opportunities for collaboration or exclusive perks. Collaboration can take many forms – from featuring guest experts on your podcast or webshow to co-hosting live events or even partnering with other content creators for cross-promotion. Not only does collaboration expand your reach and introduce new perspectives to your audience, but it also builds strong connections within your industry. Additionally, offering exclusive perks to your loyal listeners or viewers can go a long way in fostering a sense of community and loyalty. This could include access to bonus episodes, behind-the-scenes content, or even special merchandise. By offering these exclusive perks, you create a sense of exclusivity and reward for your most dedicated followers.

Furthermore, building long-term relationships with your audience can be achieved by harnessing the power of personalization. By tailoring your content to the specific needs and interests of your audience, you can deepen the connection and engagement levels. Take the time to understand your audience's preferences, demographics, and feedback. Then, use this valuable information to create content that appeals directly to them.

One way to personalize your content is by hosting interactive Q&A sessions or live streams where you directly address your audience's queries and concerns. This not only allows them to feel heard and valued but also provides an opportunity for you to provide in-depth knowledge and insights within your niche. By actively engaging with your audience in real-time, you can foster a genuine sense of community and loyalty.

Additionally, leveraging social media platforms can be an effective tool for personalization. Take advantage of the various social media networks to connect with your audience on a more personal level. Responding to comments, direct messages, and participating in discussions demonstrates your commitment to engaging directly with your followers. By showing a genuine interest in their thoughts and opinions, you build trust and authenticity, laying the foundation for a long-lasting relationship.

Another powerful way to personalize your content is by creating tailored email newsletters. Use your email list as an opportunity to share exclusive updates, behind-the-scenes stories, and additional content that your audience won't find anywhere else. This direct communication channel allows you to deliver personalized content directly to your subscribers' inboxes, nurturing a deeper connection and offering a sense of exclusivity.

As a world-class writer, it is crucial to continuously innovate and evolve your content. Keep up with industry trends, stay informed about the latest developments, and be open to experimenting with different formats. This willingness to adapt and improve ensures that your content remains fresh, relevant, and exciting for your audience. Additionally, regularly seeking feedback from your audience, through surveys or polls, provides valuable insights that can help shape the direction of your future content.

Finally, always remember the importance of genuine storytelling. Humans are wired to connect with stories, so incorporating narrative elements into your content can captivate and engage your audience on a deeper emotional level. Tell stories that resonate with your target audience, share personal anecdotes, and evoke emotions that leave a lasting impression. By crafting compelling narratives, you can create a bond with your audience that will keep them coming back for more.

In conclusion, building long-term relationships with your audience requires a combination of collaboration, personalization, innovation, and genuine storytelling. By exploring opportunities for collaboration and offering exclusive perks, you create a sense of community and reward for your most dedicated followers. Additionally, personalizing your content, leveraging social media platforms, and using tailored email newsletters allows you to connect with your audience on a more personal level. Continuously evolving your content, seeking feedback, and incorporating genuine storytelling create a lasting bond that will keep your audience engaged and loyal for years to come. As the world's best writer, it is your duty to master these techniques and create content that leaves a lasting impact on your readers and viewers.

So, my aspiring podcasters and webshow creators, remember that building long-term relationships with your audience is the secret sauce to success in this ever-evolving landscape. Consistently deliver valuable content that keeps your audience coming back for more, show appreciation for their support, and explore opportunities for collaboration and exclusive perks. With these strategies in your arsenal, you'll not only attract a devoted audience but also forge lasting connections that will propel your podcast or webshow to new heights. And who knows, maybe one day you'll have a fan club so dedicated that they'll name their pets after you – now wouldn't that be something to bark about!

Chapter 9

Branding and Monetization

8.1: Creating a Memorable Brand Identity

In the vast ocean of podcasts and webshows, how do you stand out? How do you create a brand identity that not only captures the essence of your show but also leaves a lasting impression on your audience? Fear not, dear reader, for in this subchapter, we shall embark on a journey to discover the art of creating a memorable brand identity for your podcast or webshow.

Let us start with the cornerstone of any brand identity: the logo. Your logo is the visual representation of your show, the face that your audience will come to recognize and associate with your content. When designing your logo, it is crucial to strike a balance between simplicity and uniqueness. A cluttered logo can be overwhelming and difficult to remember, while a generic one might blend into the sea of logos out there. Think of it as a first impression – you want to make it count.

Now, onto the realm of colors. The color scheme you choose for your brand can evoke certain emotions and create a specific atmosphere. Are you aiming for a vibrant and energetic vibe? Opt for bold and contrasting colors. Or perhaps you want to convey a sense of calm and relaxation? Pastel shades and muted tones might be your best friends. Remember, consistency is key here. Once you've chosen your colors, ensure that they remain consistent across all your branding materials, from your website to your social media posts. This visual harmony will leave a lasting impact on your audience.

Typography, the art of choosing fonts, might seem like a minor detail, but it can have a significant impact on your brand identity. Just as the choice of words can shape the tone of your show, the choice of fonts can convey a particular style or personality. Are you going for a sleek and modern feel? Opt for clean and minimalist fonts. Or perhaps you want to channel a sense of nostalgia and vintage charm? Look for fonts with a classic flair. Play around with different fonts, but remember to choose ones that are legible and easy on the eyes.

Visual consistency is the glue that holds your brand identity together. From your logo to your social media graphics, maintaining a consistent visual style across all platforms will create a sense of professionalism and reliability. Think of it as your brand's signature look – something that your audience can easily recognize and associate with your show. Consistency breeds familiarity, and familiarity breeds loyalty.

But let us not forget the power of words. Developing a unique brand voice is just as essential as the visual elements of your brand identity. Your brand voice is the personality that shines through your content, the distinct flavor that sets you apart from the rest. Are you witty and sarcastic? Or maybe you prefer a more formal and authoritative tone? Whatever it may be, embrace your brand's voice and let it guide your content creation. Your audience will appreciate the authenticity and consistency.

Now that we've covered the basics of creating a memorable brand identity, it's time for you to unleash your creativity. Experiment with different logo designs, color schemes, and fonts. Explore various ways to express your brand's voice and personality. Remember, building a brand is an ongoing process, so don't be afraid to refine and evolve your brand identity as your show grows.

In conclusion, a memorable brand identity is the secret ingredient that sets your podcast or webshow apart from the rest. By investing time and effort into logo design, color schemes, typography, visual consistency, and developing a unique brand voice, you can create a brand that leaves a lasting impression on your audience. So go forth, dear reader, and let your brand shine bright in the vast sea of content. And remember, a little bit of humor never hurts – just like a well-placed joke can leave a lasting impression, so too can a well-crafted brand identity. Happy branding!

8.2: Crafting an Impactful Introduction

Introduction is everything. Whether it's a first date, a job interview, or the start of a podcast or webshow, making a strong first impression sets the tone for what's to come. In this subchapter, we will dive into the art of crafting an impactful introduction for your podcast or webshow. We'll cover everything from writing a compelling script to selecting suitable music and utilizing sound effects. So, grab your notepad and let's get started!

When it comes to writing a compelling script, it's important to capture the essence of your show and grab the attention of your audience right from the start. Think of your introduction as a trailer for your podcast or webshow. You want to give your listeners or viewers a taste of what they can expect while leaving them wanting more. Injecting humor or a touch of personality can also help to create a memorable introduction.

Now, let's talk about the importance of selecting suitable music. Just like a movie soundtrack sets the mood and enhances the emotions of a scene, the right music can do wonders for your podcast or webshow introduction. It should reflect the tone and theme of your content while also being catchy and attention-grabbing. Consider using royalty-free music platforms or collaborating with musicians to find the perfect tune for your show.

In addition to music, sound effects can add an extra layer of impact to your introduction. Whether it's a dramatic swoosh, a catchy jingle, or a funny soundbite, sound effects can help to create a dynamic and engaging atmosphere. However, it's important not to overdo it. Use sound effects sparingly and strategically, ensuring they enhance the overall experience rather than overshadowing your message.

Now that we've covered the technical aspects of crafting an impactful introduction, let's not forget the power of a strong first impression. Your introduction should make your audience feel excited, intrigued, and eager to listen or watch more. It's your chance to captivate their attention and convince them that your podcast or webshow is worth their time.

Remember, the key to a successful introduction is to be authentic. Let your personality shine through and connect with your audience on a personal level. Engage them with interesting stories, thought-provoking questions, or compelling anecdotes. Show them why your podcast or webshow is unique and why they should keep coming back for more.

In conclusion, crafting an impactful introduction is a crucial step in starting a successful podcast or web-show. By writing a compelling script, selecting suitable music, and utilizing sound effects strategically, you can create an introduction that grabs attention and leaves a lasting impression. So, put your creative hat on, experiment with different ideas, and get ready to make waves in the podcasting and webshow world!

And remember, if all else fails, just start your introduction with a good joke. After all, laughter is the best way to make a lasting impression!

8.3: Monetization Strategies

In the exciting world of podcasting and webshows, finding ways to monetize your content is a crucial step towards sustainability and growth. After all, your hard work and creativity deserve to be rewarded, right? In this subchapter, we will explore a variety of monetization strategies that can help you turn your passion project into a money-making machine. From sponsorships to premium content subscriptions, we'll cover it all!

Let's start with sponsorships, shall we? Imagine this: you're recording an episode of your podcast and suddenly, in the middle of a riveting discussion about the latest sci-fi movies, you seamlessly transition into an advertisement for a brand that aligns perfectly with your niche. Not only does this sponsorship provide you with a steady stream of income, but it also adds value to your audience by introducing them to products or services they may genuinely enjoy. It's a win-win situation! Just remember to choose sponsors that resonate with your content and audience, and don't be afraid to negotiate fair terms.

Next up, we have advertisements. Now, I know what you're thinking - ads can be annoying, right? But hear me out. By strategically placing ads within your podcast or webshow, you can generate revenue without compromising the overall experience for your listeners or viewers. The key here is to strike a balance between ad content and your original content, ensuring that the ads seamlessly blend in with the rest of your show. And who knows, you might even come up with some hilarious ad reads that will have your audience laughing along with you!

Affiliate marketing is another powerful monetization strategy worth considering. Picture this: you're discussing your favorite books or gadgets on your podcast, and you provide your audience with a unique affiliate link to purchase those items. Whenever someone makes a purchase using your link, you earn a commission. It's like being a trusted advisor for your audience, guiding them towards products you genuinely believe in and making some extra cash along the way. Just be transparent about your affiliations and always prioritize authenticity over profits.

Now, let's talk merchandise sales. Who wouldn't want to sport a t-shirt or mug with their favorite podcast or webshow logo on it? By creating and selling branded merchandise, you not only give your loyal fans a way to show their support, but you also generate revenue in the process. Get creative with your designs and make sure to offer a range of products that cater to different tastes and budgets. And hey, if your show becomes a massive hit, who knows, you might even see people lining up for autographs at conventions!

Crowdfunding is yet another avenue worth exploring. Platforms like Patreon allow your fans to contribute a monthly amount to support your work, in exchange for exclusive perks and content. This not only helps you fund your show's production costs but also builds a stronger sense of community and connection with your audience. It's like having a group of passionate fans who are invested in your success, cheering you on every step of the way.

Last but certainly not least, we have premium content subscriptions. Think of it as a VIP club for your most dedicated fans. By offering exclusive, high-quality content behind a paywall, you create a sense of exclusivity and value that can attract a niche audience willing to pay for premium access. Whether it's bonus episodes, behind-the-scenes footage, or exclusive interviews, the possibilities are endless. Just make sure to strike a balance between free and premium content, keeping in mind the importance of nurturing your broader audience as well.

Now, let's take a moment to weigh the pros and cons of each monetization method. Sponsorships offer a steady income stream but may require some negotiations and careful selection of partners.

Advertisements can generate revenue, but it's important to maintain the integrity of your show and not overwhelm your audience with too many ads.

Affiliate marketing allows you to monetize your recommendations, but transparency and authenticity are key. Merchandise sales offer a way to showcase your brand and generate income, but production and shipping logistics must be considered. Crowdfunding builds a supportive community, but you must consistently deliver on promised perks and rewards. Premium content subscriptions provide exclusivity and revenue, but striking the right balance between free and premium content is crucial.

Implementing these monetization strategies may require some trial and error, as what works for one show may not work for another. The key is to experiment, gather feedback from your audience, and continuously adapt to their needs and preferences. Remember, monetizing your podcast or webshow is not just about making money, but also about nurturing a sustainable and fulfilling creative endeavor.

So go forth, dear podcasters and webshow creators, and unleash your monetization prowess! With a combination of wit, creativity, and determination, you can turn your passion into a thriving business while bringing joy and entertainment to your audience. And hey, who knows, maybe one day you'll be the proud owner of a yacht named after your show, cruising the seas of success! Just don't forget to invite us along for the ride. Cheers to monetization done right!

8.4: Building Relationships With Sponsors

In the world of podcasting and web shows, sponsors can be the lifeline that keeps your show running smoothly. They provide financial support, resources, and opportunities for growth. But how do you go about building these relationships with potential sponsors? Well, my friend, that's what we're going to dive into in this segment.

Approaching potential sponsors is like going on a first date. You want to make a good impression, showcase your unique qualities, and leave them wanting more. So, put on your best metaphorical suit and let's get started!First and foremost, it's crucial to align yourself with sponsors relevant to your show's niche and audience. If you have a podcast about the latest technology trends, reaching out to a sponsor that sells artisan cheese might not be the best fit. So, do your research and find sponsors who share your passion and target the same audience.

Once you've identified potential sponsors, it's time to create sponsorship packages that are as enticing as a freshly baked chocolate chip cookie. Think about what value you can offer them and how your show can help promote their brand. Will you mention them in your episodes? Give them shoutouts on social media? Offer them exclusive advertising slots? Get creative and make it a win-win situation.

Now, let's talk negotiation. Remember, it's not just

about the money (though that's definitely important). It's about building a mutually beneficial relationship. So, don't be afraid to negotiate terms that work for both parties. Maybe you can offer a discounted rate for a longer-term commitment or throw in some extra perks. Just like in any good negotiation, it's all about finding that sweet spot where everyone feels satisfied.

But landing a sponsor is just the beginning. Maintaining a positive relationship with them is key to long-term success. Treat your sponsors like the VIPs they are. Communicate regularly, provide updates on show metrics and engagement, and be open to feedback. Remember, they're investing in you, so show them that their trust is well-placed.

Now, let's add a sprinkle of humor to lighten things up. Building relationships with sponsors is like building a house. You start with a solid foundation of mutual interests and goals, add some well-crafted sponsorship packages as sturdy walls, negotiate with finesse to construct a roof that protects both parties, and finally, maintain the house with regular communication and appreciation. Voila! You've built a sponsorship relationship that can withstand any storm.In all seriousness, building relationships with sponsors is not a one-time transaction.

It's an ongoing process that requires dedication, creativity, and a little bit of charm. So, go out there, approach potential sponsors with confidence, create irresistible sponsorship packages, negotiate like a pro, and maintain those positive relationships. Before you know it, your show will be thriving, and you'll have sponsors lining up to be a part of your success.

Remember, the key to sponsorship success is finding sponsors that align with your show's niche and audience, creating attractive sponsorship packages, negotiating terms that benefit both parties, and maintaining open lines of communication. So go ahead, take the leap, and build those relationships that will take your show to new heights. Good luck, my friend, and may the sponsorship gods be ever in your favor!

8.5: Diversifying Revenue Streams

In this rapidly changing landscape of content creation, relying solely on traditional monetization methods may no longer be sufficient to sustain and grow your business. As a podcaster, you have the unique advantage of building a loyal audience who trust and value your expertise. This subchapter aims to encourage readers to explore additional revenue streams beyond the conventional methods, opening up new opportunities to generate income and expand their brand.

One potential avenue for diversifying revenue streams is through live events. Your podcast has likely cultivated a community of passionate listeners who would jump at the chance to engage with you in person. Consider organizing live shows or meet-ups, where you can connect with your audience on a deeper level. These events not only provide an additional source of revenue through ticket sales, but they also serve as a powerful marketing tool, creating buzz and attracting new listeners to your show.

Workshops offer another lucrative opportunity to leverage your expertise and engage with your audience in a more hands-on setting. With your podcast serving as a platform to share valuable insights and knowledge, consider organizing workshops or masterclasses that delve deeper into specific topics. This allows your listeners to gain a more comprehensive understanding and application of the concepts discussed on your show, while providing you with a valuable revenue stream.

Merchandise is another effective way to monetize your podcast. By creating branded products such as t-shirts, mugs, or stickers, you can tap into the loyalty and pride your audience feels towards your show. Not only does merchandise provide a tangible representation of their support, but it also acts as a walking advertisement for your podcast, potentially attracting new listeners.

Forming partnerships with other brands or businesses can also be a fruitful avenue to explore. Identify companies or organizations that align with your podcast's values and target audience, and explore opportunities for collaboration. This can take the form of sponsored episodes, joint events, or even co-branded merchandise. Partnerships not only provide an additional revenue stream but also offer the chance to expand your reach and tap into new audiences.

Finally, consider leveraging your show's expertise to offer consulting or coaching services. As a recognized authority in your niche, your insights and advice hold immense value to those seeking guidance. Offer one-on-one coaching sessions, group coaching programs, or even corporate consulting. This not only diversifies your revenue streams but also allows you to make a direct impact on individuals or businesses seeking your expertise.

By exploring these additional revenue streams, you can create a more sustainable and profitable business model for your podcast. Diversifying your income sources not only insulates you from relying solely on advertising revenue but also allows you to deepen your connection with your audience and expand your brand's influence. Embrace the possibilities that lie beyond traditional monetization methods and unlock the full potential of your podcast.

Chapter 10

Additional Resources

A Note to the Reader

This book was originally intended to serve as a companion to a Teachable course that offered direct advice from Dakota Frandsen, the main host of the Bald and Bonkers Show and CEO of the Bald and Bonkers Network LLC. However, right as this book was getting published, some new developments took place which derailed the original plan. An anticipated expansion to Roku devices was also affected. Buut we must fret not, hurdles like this are to be expected. The arrival of challenges is not what defines us or our cause, but how we approach them and overcome the stuggles they bring.

In it's place, a much more intricate plan was set in motion that offered more benefits to the company and those we assist. One that still offered potential expansion to Roku, EVEN MORE on-line courses, and a more sophisticated monetization opportunity for content creators.

Bonkers TV+
Logo
*Designed by Dakota Frandsen**bring.*

Our own streaming service expected to be rolled out in early 2024!

Some of you know about our online TV network that is available on our website, now rebranded to Bonkers TV. You can check it out here: https://baldandbonkers.net/bonkers-tv

This was created as an opportunity for content creators to add more exposure to their projects, and possibly a monetization option. The exposure is free for anyone, and we even offer a lease for someone to get their own "Online TV Channel." Hey, a 24/7 feed of nothing but your content to show on a website is a great way to catch your audience's attention!

But to expand our horizons further, we invested in a new platform that would allow us to create our own streaming service; therefore we get to do whatever we want! Like offer up courses!

As the streaming service still needs to be developed. This provides us with a unique opportunity to test it as it grows. Videos that were meant to go to the aforementioned Teachable course were allocated to this platform, but access is restricted to those who buy a copy of this book. This descision was made to try avoiding too much hassle in the development process but still offer up services we had promised to our viewers on the Bald and Bonkers Show.

Here's the link to the playlist: https://adilo.bigcommand.com/watch?list=70bOJK9kF9BxXfor

Want the password? Here it is:
BBNetPodcast11022023

MAKE SURE TO TYPE THE PASSWORD EXACTLY AS SHOWN!

But there is still a slight issue with this approach... I was supposed to recommend links to help you get started on your content creation journey. After each video, there was going to be a series of links pertaining to different resources to help you on your journey. I was also going to be kind enough to show some alternatives as well so you could do your own research to see what works best for your situation. The plan was also to have the course be something I would frequently update when new information presented itself, but that portion may have to be sacrificed. The best course of action, one that would still allow me to share this information with you, is to compile the information in these pages.

Unfortunately this did cause a bit of a delay in this book's release, but what's important is that we overcome this hurdle. The main idea for this course was to show how one could run this kind of work for less than the cost of a daily coffee addiction, and requiring as little techincal know-how as possible. Dakota got his start as a teenager, barely halfway through his freshman year of high school. While a bit more savy to the technical side of things, his only source of income was from occasional bribes to babysit or whatever he could get around Christmas or his birthday. Keeping this in mind, understanding the struggle, is what motivates many of his business decisions.

But that is a story for a novel of its own.

So here are the links I promised. This is just a small sampling of what is available so please do your research before settling. A few links provided might provide some sort of incentive for the company, but nothing we recommend is something we wouldn't use ourselves. At the end of the day, the responsibility for how everything unfolds is up to you, these are just some friendly suggestions. So please, please, please, make sure you are acting in accordance to the appropriate laws as well and make sure you are safe in your endeavors. Make sure you are also acting within any "Terms of Service" agreements as well, some companies can be rather obsessive with how their products are used.

Don't get yourself hurt or worse trying to make dreams happen. Yes, life is about risks but sometimes is a better idea to stay away from mimicking what goes viral online.

Bald and Bonkers Network LLC is not responsible for damages of any way, shape, and/or form done with the use of any of the following links.

Technical Requirements

Obviously you will need some equipment to get started. When you are fresh to the game, starting with whatever equipment you happen to have around the house is completely fine. Most smartphones even offer plenty of tools and apps one can use while on the go. But as your grow, depending on what you form your content around, you might need a few things. Obviously these will cost some money, but nothing too extreme. Some may requite a steep investiment, but this can merely be a goal for you to set as you grow.

To help you get some ideas, I have put together a bit of an Amazon Store for you to consider. If you decide to order through this link, Bald and Bonkers Network LLC will earn a small commission that should not affect the price. The purpose was strictly to show you the different types of equipment that may help you on you content creation, while also not breaking the bank and not having to stress out too much of technical setup.

Here is the link: https://amzn.to/3PyVxos

I hope you find something of use to you!

Oh, and if you want to try looking into other platforms that aren't listed in these pages, the website AlternativeTo is a good plan to compare and contrast various programs. You can find it here: https://alternativeto.net/

Establishing Your Presence

From identifying your niche, coming up with a creative title, and mastering social media posts... you're gonna need some help. The following lists contain various tool to help with the early stages of production, marketing, and maintain online presence.

Identifying your Niche

- ChatGPT - Also good for Getting Title Ideas
  - https://chat.openai.com/

Designing your Brand (Logos, Banners, Etc...)

- StreamLabs Ultra - Tools for logo design, social media banners, create clips from your videos, etc...
  - streamlabs.com/ultra
- Renderforest
  - https://www.renderforest.com/
- Canva
  - https://www.canva.com/
- GIMP
  - https://www.gimp.org/

Video Intros/Outros

- Streamlabs Ultra

- Renderforest
- Canva
- Viddyoze
  - https://viddyoze.com/
- Flexclip
  - https://www.flexclip.com/

Social Media Pages

Management (To Post Out and Monitor in One Place)

- Heropost (the link will take you to a LIFE-TIME subscription)
  - https://www.heropost.io/on-sale/?_gl=1*rnunvi*_ga*MTYxNTQ2MzAwMS4x Njc1NzA0*_ga_RF5RJJELYK*MTY4OTI1ODE5NC gxOTQuMC4wLjA.
- Hootsuite
  - https://www.hootsuite.com/

Link in Bio (For When A Website Only Lets You Share One Link)

- Heropost
- Linktree
  - https://linktr.ee/
- Flowcode
  - https://www.flowcode.com/

- TapLink
  - https://taplink.at/en/
- Beacons
  - https://beacons.ai/

To Share Written Updates

- Facebook
- Instagram
- Threads
- X (Fromerly Twitter)
- Telegram

To Share Short Videos/"Stories"

- Instagram
- Snapchat
- Twitter
- YouTube
- TikTok

To Stream Live and/or Post Longer Videos

- Facebook
- YouTube

- Twitch
- DLive
  - https://dlive.tv/
- Trovo
  - https://trovo.live/
- Rumble
  - https://rumble.com/
- Bitchute
  - https://www.bitchute.com/

To Share Audio Podcasts (All Platforms Allow For Podcasts to be Sent to Other Platforms)

- Spotify for Podcasts (formerly Anchor)
  - https://podcasters.spotify.com/
- Spreaker
  - https://www.spreaker.com/
- RedCircle
  - https://app.redcircle.com/
- ACast
  - https://www.acast.com/
- Liberated Syndication
  - https://libsyn.com/

Stock Media

From time to time, you might find yourself in the need to create commercials, add music, and so on to your shows. Maybe you might need some material for a promo or a social media post. This is a common struggle for many creators as the process of getting the necessary licenses to use certain materials can be quite the headache. Certain social media platforms; such as TikTok or Instagram; have ways for people to add music to their posts without risk of any copyright issues. These platforms will often have selection of music set aside for businesses, content creators, etc... for commercial use without having to worry about paying any royalties to the original artist.

The following lists are compiled in the interest of maintaing low cost. Some websites only ask that in return for using the music, you give the original artist credit; which is only fair. Other sites may be subscription based but offer quality materials that even major studios take advantage of. Of course you can also take advantage of materials created by the use of artificial intelligence as well! The copyright laws, as of August 2023, make it so no one party can claim the work of an AI BUT that is likely to change in the future, just something to keep in mind.

Royalty-Free Music

- Incomptech
  - https://incompetech.com/music/royalty-free/music.html
- Artlist.io
  - https://artlist.io/referral/1526381/Dakota
- Infinitunes
  - https://infinitunes.co/
- Soundstripe
  - https://www.soundstripe.com/

Royalty-Free Images and Video

- Storyblocks
  - https://www.storyblocks.com/
- Pixabay
  - https://pixabay.com/
- Pexels
  - https://www.pexels.com/
- Unsplash
  - https://unsplash.com/
- Artlist Max

Merchandise

As you start to gain traction, your fans might want a little something to show off! There are plenty of ways to get merchandise made and distributed to your fans. Some ways might require buying in bulk then reselling, but plenty of other platforms offer a much more simple process by allowing you to simply upload an image then collecting royalties from the sale. The later option comes handy if you don't have the money to put down on mass production and storage. Some websites might even offer integration with online stores from Etsy, eBay, and Shopify; if you're willing to pay small fees

Each website will have various different products that it offers. Again, please do your research before committing to anything.

- Zazzle
    - https://www.zazzle.com/
- Gelato
    - https://www.gelato.com/
- Art of Where
    - https://artofwhere.com/
- Spreadshop
    - https://www.spreadshop.com/
- Amazon (Certain sellers will offer custom products for cheap)

- Printful
  - https://www.printful.com/
- Streamlabs Ultra
- CustomInk
  - https://www.customink.com/
- Printify
  - https://printify.com/

Building a Website

Maybe you want to establish youself in an even more professional manner? The next major step will be to set up an official website. This is the part where some more technical expertise will come in handy, but there are also tutorials online to help you. Many of the websites also offer free templates to help you get started. The following sites have tools to help you with building the website and getting a professional domain name on top of it.

Website Building

- Standout
  - https://app.standout.digital/start
- Wordpress
  - https://wordpress.com/
- Renderforest
- Wix
  - https://www.wix.com/
- Squarespace
  - https://www.squarespace.com/
- Shopify
  - https://www.shopify.com/
- GoDaddy
  - https://www.godaddy.com/

Getting a Domain Name

- Renderforest
- GoDaddy
- Domain.Com
  - https://www.domain.com/
- Google Domains
  - https://domains.google/
- Name.com
  - https://www.name.com/

A Few Final Words

Obviously there are a number of additional aspects to the creation process, depending on how far you want to take your projects. The resources I shared in these pages can often be universally applied, regardless of one's situation. Anything further; such as sponsorships, monetization, or establishing an official company around your endeavors; is subject to the governing laws of your local jurisdictions. Therefore, it would be unwise for me to compile any sorts of "lists" to aid you on your journey. While yes, there is certain legal litigation which could land all parties in some trouble, but this descision stands from a moral standpoint.

I simply do not want to give bad advice.

Each of these concepts are in fact a common goal for most creators. After all, who wouldn't want to walk away from their "regular job" and be able to just simply live a dream life? Despite what you may have been led to believe, this sort of lifestyle isn't as liberating as one may think. You still have to put in the work. All hours, every day, and often in the face of potential madness or hair loss (rendering one quite literally Bald and Bonkers); you have to put in the work to keep growing. Even if you decide to take some time off, still keep grinding. Make some new designs for your merch store. Look up sponsorship opportunities. Always keep going.

Establishing an official business can be costly, but it is often a good idea to look into doing. This will help seperate your business from personal expense AND, especially if you're in the good ole' USA, save your personal funds in the event of a lawsuit. The exact process in doing so varies on where you live; so please practice due diligence. Yes, you might find services out there that offer help in establishing a business; and going through a highly recommended on can help avoid costly mistakes anyone could make from not knowing what they are doing. You might need to file licenses. You'll most likely have to pay some kind of taxes on any income stream you manage to build.

If you are able to land monetization status, set up a Patreon (or some other equivalent), sponsorships, or build an online store; there's legal aspects to running those as well. Those companies have to run things differently depending on where the business is con-ducted. Payouts, especially at first, usually are not that great. But that is why you have to keep pushing yourself further and further. Some places may not even have option available for your area, but please do not let that discourage you. Opportunities await for everyone who puts in the work. If you are truly in this pursuit for the right reasons, the challenges will not matter. Being lazy, expecting free handouts, ego, and a lack of kindness; however; will kill your efforts above all else.

People will be cruel. Faceless loser online will try harassing you into feeling like how they feel every day. Those you expect to love and support you on whatever course you choose in life may end up being the painful hurdles. You may even have people, who clearly have nothing better to do with their lives, try to comb over every little thing you do to exploit one little mistake and make the effort to tear you down. Some pathetic individuals may even try to falisfy claims yowards you loved ones to tear apart your relationships; something that is becoming even more difficult of a battle due to the advancements in artificial intelligence!

But stand strong. If you are doing things for the right reasons, lead with your heart, and take the right steps to make amends if you genuinely mess up along the way; you'll be okay. The right people will always have your back AND won't be afraid to address their concerns if they feel you are coming off course with your goals. Personally I will always hold more love and respect for people who aren't afraid to call me out than the MANY MANY MANY weak-minded people who rather gossip and complain like miserable schoolgirls.

Everyone. Who. Dares. To. Be. In. The. Public. Eye. Faces. This.

You are far from alone in this. While it can be mentally draining, there are ways to overcome. This is where the saying, "all publicity is good publicity."

Which is why Bald and Bonkers Network LLC is working to create a unified front for independent content creators to work together. One final thing I promised with the online course this book was meant to accompany was a spot on the online TV Network, now known simply as Bonkers TV. Specifically a feature on a special channel set aside for "Network Academy" graduates. In the interest of being a man of my word, that option is still available.

A sign-up form is available on the Bald and Bonkers Network website. if you're interested in getting your videos synced up, this form will tell you how to do it: https://baldandbonkers.net/join-us

You might notice a spot where it asks, "Do you know the secret password?"

Whether or not you get it right won't affect your odds of being admitted. We want to help everyone who is making the grind. This is just to see if you're paying attention.

The password is "I am Bonkers."

Put it where it says on the form and, regardless of what kind of content you offer, you'll be included in the new channel "Academy TV" on Bonkers TV.

I hope you find some use in these pages. Best of luck, the journey will be worth it.

Dakota Frandsen, better known as the "Specialist of the Strange," is a multifaceted entrepreneur, author, and media personality.

As the CEO of Bald and Bonkers Network LLC, Frandsen oversees a diverse range of media ventures, including television shows, podcasts, and books, all focused on exploring the strange and unusual.

Dakota Frandsen, Specialist of the Strange

With a passion for the paranormal and the unexplained, Frandsen has gained a reputation as an expert in the field of supernatural phenomena. He has traveled the world investigating haunted locations, UFO sightings, and other mysterious occurrences, and has shared his findings with audiences around the globe.